WIND, SUN, SOIL, SPIRIT

WIND, SUN, SOIL, SPIRIT

Biblical Ethics and Climate Change

CAROL S. ROBB

Fortress Press
Minneapolis

WIND, SUN, SOIL, SPIRIT
Biblical Ethics and Climate Change

Scripture quotations are from the New Revised Standard Version Bible, copyright © 1989 by the Division of Christian Education of the National Council of the Churches of Christ in the U.S.A. Used by permission. All rights rserved.

Cover image: Olive Orchard, Violet Soil, Vincent van Gogh (1853–1890 Dutch), Van Gogh Museum, Amsterdam, Netherlands / Veer
Cover design: Laurie Ingram
Book design: PerfecType, Nashville, TN

Library of Congress Cataloging-in-Publication Data

Robb, Carol S.
   Wind, sun, soil, spirit : biblical ethics and climate change / Carol S. Robb.
      p. cm.
   ISBN 978-0-8006-9706-8 (alk. paper)
   1. Global warming—Religious aspects—Christianity. 2. Environmental ethics. 3. Ethics in the Bible. 4. Bible. N.T.—Criticism, interpretation, etc. I. Title.
   BR115.G58R63 2010
   220.8'36373874—dc22
                                                          2009036767

The paper used in this publication meets the minimum requirements of American National Standard for Information Sciences — Permanence of Paper for Printed Library Materials, ANSI Z329.48-1984.

Manufactured in the U.S.A.

14 13 12 11 10 1 2 3 4 5 6 7 8 9 10

CONTENTS

Part Two
Reading the Bible and Doing Ethics

Part Three
Biblical Social Ethics and the Kingdom of Oil

PREFACE

As the new millennium was breaking in, Christopher Lind, then of St. Andrew's College in Saskatoon, Saskatchewan, Canada, called to invite me to resource a consultation on climate change organized by the World Council of Churches' Climate Change Program. I was eager—and unprepared. I knew something about the phenomena associated with global climate change because Bill Somplatsky-Jarman had been doing education on the topic for the Presbyterian Church USA and the National Council of Churches for more than fifteen years. David Hallman, the coordinator of the Climate Change Program, channeled background material my way. My challenge was to contribute a theological-ethical perspective to representatives of the WCC who would be observers at the then upcoming Sixth Session of the Conference of the Parties (COP6) to the U.N. Framework Convention on Climate Change at The Hague, November 2000.

To the Saskatoon Consultation I delivered this message: though the people of the Mediterranean world knew nothing about climate change as far as we know, the Bible, in this case the New Testament texts, are surprisingly relevant to our debate over climate change policies. This book is an amplification of that initial message.

The questions that ground the development of this book are these:

How are people of the world talking about decreasing the greenhouse gas emissions affecting global climate? I'll address this question by describing the Kyoto Treaty and its flexibility mechanisms. The Kyoto Treaty governs emissions of its signatories through 2012. While the United States is not a signatory of Kyoto, the current administration and legislative branches are exhibiting genuine openness to engaging debate over the next treaty. So hope is in the air. And the issues that fed into Kyoto are going to be with us in the next treaties, so we had better understand them so we can help shape them.

How do people of good will identify the moral issues triggered by policy debate and design? What makes a climate change policy right or wrong? I will show you why and how *every* mode of moral discourse ethicists typically use to answer this question has to be employed to get at the moral meaning of the policy debates.

Of what significance to climate policies might it be that a people considers itself Christian? The choices of climate policies being considered and made at this historical juncture are likely to affect the meaning of human life and the complexity of ecologies for decades and centuries. The climatologists employed by the United Nations do not want the responsibility of making these decisions, and good for them! The possible futures depicted by the different paths we can choose are quite different. Shouldn't this discussion be as wide as we can possibly make it? Yes.

How does a religious tradition, in this case Christian, relate its particular sources, in this case the Bible with a focus on the New Testament, to a public discussion over matters that affect the whole globe? Humbly, and with as much knowledge as we can muster about the historical context the different texts emerged from and addressed. And in that historical context, it helps to identify the sociological, biological, cultural, economic, and political dynamics at play, since ecological debates are rooted in all these dynamics.

Specifically, what is the relevance of Jesus of Nazareth to climate change? Because his own audiences were largely people working the land, Jesus' hearers were quite attuned to the political and economic consequences on ecology of land ownership patterns and farm-worker labor practices. This is the level at which climate policies connect to the first-century Mediterranean world.

What is the relevance of Paul to climate change? Open question. Exciting work on Paul flowing forth during the last two decades presents a still inchoate picture of this person and his mission viewed sociologically. Nevertheless, I will formulate some questions to bring to Paul's letters, hoping to contribute to further work on his possible relevance to contemporary policy discussions.

Do the New Testament texts sharpen contemporary readers' eyes to issues very connected to climate policies? I will answer yes, if we can use sociology, cultural studies, and economic and political history to inform our reading of the texts. Then we will better be able to find analogies, or lack of them, with the contemporary world.

Should it matter to contemporary Christians what ancient texts say? It just *does* matter, whether it should or not. But I have discovered that Christian ethicists seem perennially vexed by how to responsibly use Scriptures as a source of authority. Biblical scholars on the other hand seem to be much freer to engage texts, argue with them, analyze them, and sometimes set them aside—all the more reason I would like Christian ethicists and biblical scholars to be more often cooperatively engaged in projects for the common good.

In that light, I want to acknowledge my colleagues in Biblical Studies at San Francisco Theological Seminary, the Graduate Theological Union, and the University of Massachusetts–Boston, but particularly Antoinette Clark Wire, Marvin Chaney, Bob Coote, Herman Waetjen, and Richard Horsley, whose work explicitly or implicitly graces these pages, or who urged me to just interpret the Bible the way I want, a sweet but futile benediction. Others offered gifts of a different nature.

Eleanor Scott Meyers painted the muse who guided my writing. Arthur Holder, dean of the GTU, Marilyn Matevia, and the faculty and trustees of SFTS played important roles supporting the generation of this book. Michael West of Fortress Press must be thanked for his light but clear direction, as well as Maurya Horgan, who copyedited the manuscript, and Marissa Wold, who shepherded the project. I want also to acknowledge David Robb for showing me the wind turbines, and Duncan Mayer Robb, whose generation will be inheriting the earth, and whose future I pondered as I wrote nearly every page.

PART ONE

Climate Change Policies: These Are Moral Matters

CHAPTER ONE

Climate Change
and Climate Treaties:
The Context for Deliberation

Introduction

Over twenty people were gathered together at a conference center on the shore of Lake Tahoe to get a grip on global climate change. A few volunteered to calculate our carbon footprints to see the scope of change we need to face. The carbon footprint calculator on a website constructed by a team associated with the University of California at Berkeley[1] provided our tool. We discovered that the average annual emission of carbon dioxide for Californians is thirty-four tons, compared to thirty-nine tons in the nation and eight worldwide. Climatologists tell us that we all need to get our footprints down to four or five tons per year if we are to prevent catastrophic effects of climate shifts. A no-regrets level will require an emission allowance of two tons per capita per year.

Some of the reporters calculated their footprints to be twenty-eight to forty-one tons, hovering around the state or national average. However, Margaret and her spouse walk, bike, and use public transportation when they can. Only rarely do they get in their hybrid auto and drive. They recycle paper, plastic, and glass. They buy almost all their clothing at thrift shops and catch cold water from the shower before it warms up to flush the toilet. They wash their laundry with cold water and shop at the farmers' market for much of their grocery list. Despite their conscientious attention to conservation, their carbon footprint is eighteen tons of carbon dioxide per year, about half the national or California average, but still over quadruple what it needs to be.

Similarly, Richard and his spouse have solar panels on their roof that generate electricity during the day, which the utility company buys from them at about one-third the retail price. One of their vehicles is an electric car, and the other is a hybrid. The electric car's battery is recharged, using a timer, between midnight and six in the morning, when the electric rates are lowest. Their home's windows are double-paned for insulation. They have invested in energy conservation and renewable energy, but because they've incorporated a fair amount of air travel into their year, mostly for mission purposes, their footprint is not as low as their daily habits would lead one to anticipate, at twenty-five tons of carbon dioxide per year, five or six times what it needs to be.

I live on the campus of a seminary, so I do not need to drive to work. The faculty house I occupy is built to use natural air conditioning. Eating within a food-shed of three hundred miles is almost always feasible, and gardening lightens the load on the grocery store and makes a network of food sharing with the neighbors possible and fun. My carbon footprint is nineteen tons of carbon dioxide per year, four or five times what it needs to be.

We are conscientious, aware of our responsibility to be earth citizens, living in a temperate climate with few weather extremes, and—relative to much of the world—wealthy in resources to decrease our greenhouse gas emissions. And yet the structures that provide us with energy and transportation are manufactured in the Kingdom of Oil. As conscientious as we are, we will not be able to lower our carbon footprints to the necessary four or five tons until state and federal and international policies are crafted that encourage new practices that deliver energy and transportation without using fossil fuel. At this point in time, we are prisoners in the Kingdom of Oil. How can we spring free? Our hope is lodged in treaties.

Climate Change Protocol

A just-so combination of water vapor, carbon dioxide, and other trace gases provides a natural greenhouse for planet Earth, preventing the sun's heat from totally re-radiating back into space at nightfall. It keeps our planet about sixty degrees warmer than it otherwise would be, providing a mitigating effect on swings in atmospheric temperatures from hot to cold. Life as we know it on Earth depends on this greenhouse effect. When we humans began burning coal, oil, and natural gas in great quantities during industrialization, however, we introduced levels of CO_2 in greater quantities and faster than the planet has seen for fifty million years.

The concentration of carbon dioxide has by no means been stable through the hundreds of thousands of years, according to Earth's records written in tiny air bubbles trapped in an Antarctic ice core. The natural swings in levels of CO_2 in the atmosphere have always correlated with temperature change. As CO_2 increases, temperatures rise. Anthropogenic (human-induced) CO_2 is similarly resulting in temperature increases. If nations continue along the current path, increasing emissions by 3.3 percent annually, CO_2 concentrations will likely be more than 700 parts per million (ppm) by 2100.[1] That level would represent double the current level (about 385 ppm CO_2 and, with the carbon equivalence of the other greenhouse gases, 430 ppm CO_2 eq) and much more than double the pre-industrial level of 280 ppm CO_2.[2] We would be looking at an increase of Earth's surface temperature from 2.7 to 11 degrees Fahrenheit by the end of this century.[3] We might refer to this phenomenon as global warming, except that the effects may not be experienced as warming in every location. If the polar caps melt and release fresh water into the Atlantic, the trajectory of the Gulf Stream will be affected, and the British Isles will lose its warming effect in the winter. Thus, the concern is better stated to be that of climate change.

Because different regions will be affected in different ways, motivation to curtail the burning of fossil fuels is mixed. Russia has large areas in permafrost that would become suitable for agriculture as a result of climate change. Russia also has large fossil fuel reserves, the sale of which would benefit its foreign exchange. Motivation to curtail use of fossil fuels is low. Similarly, the OPEC nations (Organization of Petroleum Exporting Countries) export petroleum and natural gas. Saudi Arabia and Kuwait control one-third of the oil reserves of the OPEC nations, and oil accounts for their foreign earnings. So the world may not see cooperation from OPEC nations in the effort to decrease the use of fossil fuels. Similarly, the United States, by far the largest emitter of CO_2, is the world's largest producer of coal, oil, and gas, even though it is a net importer of energy products. Energy producers thus view efforts to decrease the use of fossil fuels as a threat. Yet the United States has a long coastline that will be affected as the sea level rises, and parts of the country experience hurricanes and other flooding, drought, and tornadoes, all of which will increase in intensity with increases in average temperatures, as the global water cycle speeds up. A sizable portion of the population in the United States is alarmed by the prospects of climate change, and this represents a pressure different from that offered by the energy producers.

On the other hand, the forty-two developing countries bound together in the Alliance of Small Island States (AOSIS) face an extreme impact from rising sea levels. Their land masses are low-lying, so that when cyclones hit, there is no place to escape. If average temperatures rise four to eight degrees in this century, the ocean level will rise at least eighteen to nineteen inches, as more glaciers and snow masses on land melt away. The island nations' survival is therefore at stake, and their representatives typically take strong stands, asking industrialized nations to decrease fossil fuel use. Along with the island nations, the European Union has played a leading role in promoting decreases in greenhouse gas emissions. While some nations within the EU are producers of oil and gas, only about half of the EU's energy needs are met domestically. Thus, these nations generally have interests in decreasing fossil fuel consumption. By virtue of their relatively successful history of private/government/environmental collaboration in reducing effluents, the EU provides strong leadership among industrialized nations in showing how such decreases can be achieved.[4]

Even among the mix of motivations of nations' leaders regarding the prospect of climate change, there has been enough consensus that the rate of change threatens the climate's balancing capacity. At the current speed of warming, trees and other flora will not have the time to migrate successfully, leading to faster loss of species. Poor air quality and the diseases that thrive in warmer climates will adversely affect human health. Beaches, populated islands, and wetlands will be inundated. A twenty-inch rise in sea level will double the global population at risk from storm surges, from about forty-five million at present to over ninety million. Droughts and floods will increase in intensity. Water supply problems in arid and semi-arid regions will be exacerbated.[5] The basis for international cooperation to lower emissions is sufficiently established to provide the impetus for some covenants and treaties. The most developed of these treaties is the Kyoto Protocol, governing emissions from 2008 to 2012, and the treaty that will follow after 2012 is at this writing being negotiated for the Copenhagen Climate Conference of December 2009. Each treaty and covenant takes into consideration what has been accomplished in prior agreements and what has succeeded or failed. In that sense the treaty process is iterative.

While the Kyoto Treaty is not the first—nor will it be the last—treaty governing international climate change policies, it is the focus of this book for two reasons. While the United States is an important neighbor in the world community, the U.S. negotiators backed out of the Kyoto Treaty because of the large impact of U.S. business and development on the climate. U.S. citizens who see themselves as earth citizens also were dismayed and ashamed by the actions of the government. Second, the issues that emerged in the Kyoto process and following are not going away. The same processes that created the need for climate treaties continue to be consequential for the earth's climate, and the mechanisms that were created in the Kyoto process have yet to be fully implemented and assessed. At this writing it is still not clear whether or how the U.S. legislative processes will empower U.S. negotiators to be good citizens. So, while the Kyoto Treaty is for a limited time frame, the policies contained within it will continue to generate moral concern for treaties to come.

The Kyoto Protocol was unanimously adopted in Kyoto, Japan, December 11, 1997, by 170 industrialized, industrializing, and nonindustrialized nations. Although the treaty provided some general directions governing the quantity of emissions to decrease and the mechanisms by which such reductions could take place, it left to future meetings the specifics of implementation. Many parties to the treaty waited for the decisions about specifics to ratify the treaty through their respective parliamentary procedures. Fifty-five ratifications were required before the treaty took effect. Even though the U.S. government, during George W. Bush's administration, withdrew from the treaty in March, 2001, the treaty nevertheless had sufficient signatories governing sufficient emissions to enter into force on February 16, 2005.[6] As of February 2007, 168 states and the European Economic Community have ratified the Protocol.[7] The rules for the Protocol's implementation were adopted at the Conference of the Parties 7 (COP7) in Marrakesh in 2001, and are called the "Marrakesh Accords."

What makes atmospheric management policy so urgent, and one for moral deliberation, is that the atmosphere is one of the global commons, such that what one nation perpetrates or tolerates will have an impact on all others. The harms of atmospheric use are shared equally, though the benefits of such use are not, and the impacts are felt differentially. More precisely, the harms of climate change fall most heavily on the nations least equipped to cope with them and least responsible for generating them.[8] The benefits of atmospheric use are enjoyed most by the industrialized nations,[9] which also disproportionately cause the problems associated with climate change. What's fair about that?

In the process of deliberating the implementation procedures, the different parties to the treaty employ the data provided by the Intergovernmental Panel on Climate Change (IPCC).[10] Those data reflect the science of climate change, as well as projections about social and economic impacts of different scenarios. The IPCC scientists, particularly those focused on mitigation of the effects of climate change, are explicit that questions of fairness (they refer to it as equity) are "in play" in considerations of climate change policy. I have introduced the question of fairness in terms of who bears the harms compared with who receives the benefits, understanding that those who receive the benefits of practices and policies should proportionally also bear the harms. However, the effort to construct climate policy has exposed additional moral dimensions, including whether we are accountable to intergenerational duties, have duties to plants and other animals, should accept differentiated obligations, have to accept responsibility for effects that could not early on be anticipated. And, by the way, are discussions of moral responsibility even relevant to treaty building? These issues will be explored more fully in chapter 2, and in chapter 3 the question of which social and ecological values should have priority in policy making.

To see climate change as provoking moral questions requires coming to grips with some strategies currently in use to stop us from doing so. The strategies include the following:

- Deny the problem. "Climate change is not really happening, or if it is it will be beneficial overall."

- Put the responsibility for not adopting climate change policies on China, India, or any other country of the two-thirds world. "Since they don't have binding obligations, we shouldn't."
- Minimize the value of the Kyoto Treaty. "Look, it's only going to result in small decreases in greenhouse gases."

And at the same time,

- Refuse to make any provisions limiting emissions binding, to maintain "voluntary" quality of all agreements.
- Trump every other consideration (inundation of Small Island Nations, increase in wild and extreme weather, increase in desertification) with the *supreme* consideration: "It would not be good for American economic life."

While at the same time,

- Ignore the fact that clean energy is a growth industry and would improve the possibility that regional economies could be less dependent on highly capitalized energy corporations and/or imported oil.

While nations' economic security is no small moral matter, it takes a multifaceted view of any nation to see what might constitute true security. The World Council of Churches provides one venue for such a multifaceted view, and, through it, the religious community has attempted to be a presence at the international meetings about climate policy. The WCC is recognized as a Non-Governmental Organization (NGO) with observer status at the meetings, and delegates to the meetings come from churches all over the world. The Climate Change Project of the World Council has conducted several consultations to inform its delegates about the science of climate change and the policies that are being considered at the negotiating sessions. At the consultations theologians reflect on the issues in light of Christian Scriptures and tradition, in addition to the expert advice and the wisdom of experience of policy analysts and church-based staff with portfolios in ecological concerns. The theological reflection has explored the depth of specific Christian perspectives and sought ways to link these particular religious communities' reflections to the worldwide common effort to craft policy governing all the nations. This essay represents one effort to make this link.

In this introductory chapter, I will describe the Kyoto Protocol in general terms, and also the three flexibility mechanisms it provides: International Emission Permit Trading, Joint Implementation, and the Clean Development Mechanism. The Protocol sets targets for reductions in emissions but does not specify how sovereign nations will achieve their reductions. Some nations, particularly in the European Union, lean heavily on policies and measures crafted in the halls of government. The United States, Canada, and Australia represent a strong tendency toward voluntarism and resistance to mandates from above. The "flexibility mechanisms" that use markets in emission allowances, carbon sequestration in sinks, and investment in "clean" technology in the developing world as ways for polluting nations to mitigate the requirements to lower greenhouse gases (GHGs) domestically were negotiated by such voluntaristic nations. As a result of the intense conflict over the outlines of these flexibility mechanisms, delegates from some southern nations have left the international meetings, the Conferences of the Parties (COPs), with the impression that such meetings are not primarily about how to lower greenhouse gas emissions but about how to make money.

The legal basis for the Kyoto Protocol was established in the United Nations Framework Convention on Climate Change (UNFCCC), adopted May 9, 1992, and entered into force March 21, 1994, with fifty ratifications. By December 2006 the Framework Convention had been ratified by 189 of the 194 UN member states.[11] The United States, though withdrawn from the Kyoto Protocol, remains a party to the FCCC.[12] The Framework Convention provided the objective that the Kyoto Protocol attempted to move toward: "stabilization of greenhouse gas concentrations in the atmosphere at a level that would prevent dangerous anthropogenic interference with the climate system." It further stated, "[S]uch a level should be achieved within a time-frame sufficient to allow eco-systems to adapt naturally to climate change, to ensure that food production is not threatened and to enable economic development to proceed in a sustainable manner."[13] The Framework Convention further stipulated that industrialized nations would voluntarily return their emissions to 1990 levels by 2000, which most failed to do. The world total CO_2 concentration in 1990 was about 355 ppm, or 400 CO_2 eq.[14]

The Intergovernmental Panel on Climate Change (IPCC), a body created in 1988 by the United Nations Environment Programme (UNEP) and the World Meteorological Organization (WMO), has provided the scientific basis for the standard "stabilization of greenhouse gases." The IPCC has undertaken four full-scale assessments of climate change: in 1990, 1995, 2001, and 2007. In addition, it has produced many smaller and more specialized reports. According to people who have been involved, each of the full assessments is a huge undertaking, involving hundreds of scientists from dozens of countries and many different disciplines as authors and as peer reviewers, including many of the most respected figures in the field.[15] These groups work over several years to produce each full assessment and subject their work to publicly documented multistage review. The IPCC assessments are the authoritative statements of scientific knowledge on climate change.

Governments maintain official control over the IPCC, and the IPCC has developed procedures that clarified and managed the boundary between its scientific and governmental aspects. The detailed work of the assessment conducted by the scientific writing teams and published in the technical summaries is supposed to be unaffected by governmental control. In the formal plenary sessions with national representatives present, the Summary for Policymakers, the shortest and most widely circulated product of each assessment report, is negotiated line by line.[16] The IPCC websites contain full texts of the writing teams' actual reports and technical summaries, as well as the "Summaries for Policymakers."[17]

The IPCC has determined that human-induced emissions of a number of gases are contributing to climate change. The major GHGs are CO_2 (carbon dioxide), CH_4 (methane), N_2O (nitrous oxide), and halocarbons such as chlorofluorocarbons (CFCs and HCFCs) and halons.[18] In the early 1990s, CO_2 accounted for about 82 percent of industrialized countries' emissions of the principal GHGs (through fossil fuel combustion—more than 95 percent—and through industrial processes). Methane constituted about 12 percent of industrialized countries' GHGs (about one-third through fossil fuel production, distribution, and combustion; about one-third through agriculture; and about one-third through waste). Nitrous oxide constituted 6 to 7 percent of such GHGs (40 percent from agriculture and about one-third from industrial processes). HFCs, PFCs, and SF_6 (hydrofluorocarbons, perfluorocarbons, and sulphur hexafluoride, respectively) constituted about 2 percent (through industrial processes, industry, consumption). Fossil fuel combustion and agricultural processes account for most of these GHGs.[19]

According to the IPCC, significant reductions of GHGs will be needed to stabilize atmospheric concentrations at relatively safe levels. CO_2 should be reduced 50 to 70 percent; CH_4 8 percent; and N_2O 50 percent.

In 1990, the base year for many parties to the Kyoto Protocol, the United States contributed 36 percent of the CO_2; the European Union, 24 percent; Russia, 17 percent; Japan, 8 percent; other Organisation for Economic Co-operation and Development (OECD) countries, 6 percent; and other countries in economic transition, 7 percent. If one looks at the per capita emissions of CO_2 of selected nations in 1990, we see figures such as these: one person in the United States creates 19.8 tons in one year; in the European Union, 8.7; Japan, 9.4; Russia, 16.1; China, 2.1; India, 0.7; Sudan, 0.2; Saudi Arabia, 10.9; Trinidad/Tobago, 10 tons. The world total per capita was 4.1 tons in 1990.[20]

Reducing the impact on the atmosphere to a no-regrets level will require an emission allowance of 2 tons per capita per year.

At the Kyoto meeting in December 1997, targets for reductions in GHGs were determined by negotiation. Only "Annex I countries" were assigned targets; these are countries that are industrialized or are Countries with Economies in Transition (CEITs). Developing countries, including India and China, are not included in Annex I and have no targets for reduction. Targets are differentiated from country to country, taking into account special factors, such as whether there have already been major transfers to renewable energy sources and hence limits on future decreases. Some countries, such as Australia, Iceland, and Norway, refused to accept reductions. But when taken together, the targets set at Kyoto would result in a 5.2 percent decrease in GHG emissions from 1990 levels by the end of the "commitment period," 2008–2012.[21] Unfortunately, even if successful in reaching these targeted reductions, they come nowhere near the 50 to 70 percent reduction in CO_2, 8 percent reduction of CH4, and 50 percent reduction of N_2O necessary to stabilize atmospheric concentrations of GHGs, according to the IPCC. However, the Kyoto Protocol did result in commitments to reverse current emission trends, and it requires of its signatories assessment practices that will facilitate the documentation of future, more stringent emission reductions.

Flexibility Mechanisms the Treaty Allows for Meeting Obligations

Recognizing climate stabilization will require tremendous changes in the way energy is produced and consumed, policymakers involved in the Kyoto Protocol focused on minimizing the economic and social costs of changing course.[22] Since energy production and use produce the lion's share of GHG emission, especially CO_2, the responsibility for achieving emission reductions will fall most heavily on the energy sector, whose infrastructure requires a lead time for innovation. "Fossil fuel combustion in power plants accounts for more than ⅓ of industrialized countries' CO_2 emissions, more than any other activity in the energy supply chain."[23] At the same time, power generation is a simpler target for government action than other CO_2 sources, such as transport. Hence, the three "flexibility mechanisms" for which the Kyoto Treaty allows are most comprehensible in the context of providing incentives for energy producers to change the modes of operation to which they are accustomed. All three mechanisms are market-based and allow developed nations party to the treaty to earn and trade emissions credits or permits to emit GHGs. Therefore, these mechanisms are about how the future consumption of the atmosphere will be distributed among the parties to the treaty and among parties who have not accepted obligations to decrease emissions under the treaty.[24] They are "tools" in the climate change treaty tool box. All three are supposed to be supplemental to the basic mechanism, in which each region makes an effort to meet its emission target through domestic action.

International emission trading. Countries with emission goals under the Kyoto Protocol can trade with one another.

Annex 1 parties are industrialized countries that aimed to return their emissions to their 1990 levels by 2000. Parties to the Kyoto Protocol then established a legally binding obligation for industrialized countries to reach these goals, based on assigned amounts, set on a country-by-country basis in Annex B of the treaty during the 2008–12 period. Some Annex 1 parties did not make a commitment (a few countries from the former Soviet Union and Turkey). Only those countries with *assigned amounts* under Annex B can participate in emission trading. They are referred to as Annex B parties or countries.[25]

One assigned amount unit (AAU) allows one ton of carbon equivalent emissions.[26]

Emission trading is provided for in Article 17 of the Protocol. It requires (1) a quantified objective (in parts per million CO_2 for the whole earth, and which to date has not been set); (2) requires countries to prepare national inventories of their

GHG emissions; (3) determines a limit or cap on total emissions for a nation; (4) translates allowed emissions into permits; and (5) creates a market in which these permits can be traded. It then requires measuring emissions during the commitment period, accurate monitoring of all the emission sources covered by the regime, tracking the assigned amount units (AAUs, or the emission permits) through an effective national registry. Emission sources that cannot be reliably monitored should not participate in the regime.[27]

Emission permit trading is a way of creating a market in greenhouse gas emissions where there has been none, and where firms have been releasing their emissions into the global commons, the atmosphere, without having to pay for the temporary use for storage of emissions. After putting a price on the emissions, firms then calculate whether they can do business better by changing their technologies and practices to decrease the cost of using the atmospheric commons. If they hold permits and are able to decrease their emissions below what the permits allow, the remaining permits may be banked for the future or sold to another firm that is unable to decrease their emissions to their assigned amount. New industries have to acquire permits, and so a market develops and entrepreneurs can make money by reducing emissions.[28]

International emission trading is ecologically effective only when the total emissions the permits represent is lower than the existing level of emissions, only when firms are not so powerful as to minimize the price of traded permits, and when producers are prevented from hoarding permits to prevent market entry by competitors.

Countries, not companies, are responsible for meeting the Kyoto objectives. Countries may allocate permits, part of their assigned amount, to companies through free distribution (grandfathering), through auctioning, or both. Santiago de Chile discovered a benefit of "grandfathering." Registration and control of emissions from point sources permitted the identification of previously undisclosed sources of pollution.[29] Negotiating the rights and duties that come with allocating permits is complex and controversial. The impetus for emission trading is trust and experience in market mechanisms for lowering the cost of compliance with emission targets, below what could be achieved using policies and measures (PAMs) domestically alone.

Joint Implementation. Annex B countries can finance projects for lowering emissions in other Annex B countries and get credit for them.

Article 6 of the Protocol allows for a project-based system under which one Annex B country can receive credit for emissions-reducing activities it finances in another Annex B country. The use of Joint Implementation (JI), as with emissions permit trading, must be supplemental to domestic actions. The type of emissions permits used in JI are emissions reduction units (ERUs) generated by the host country, who converts some of their AAUs (assigned amount units) to ERUs on a one-to-one basis and transfers them to the country sponsoring the project.[30] One ERU also allows one ton of carbon-equivalent emissions. Joint Implementation assumes foreign financing.

JI is designed to allow for countries without low-cost reduction opportunities to invest in lower-cost abatement in other countries and gain credit toward their own commitments.[31]

Clean Development Mechanism. Annex 1 parties may invest in emission abatement projects in non-Annex 1 nations.

The Clean Development Mechanism (CDM) is provided for by Article 12 of the Kyoto Protocol and is a scheme of project-based activities where Annex 1 parties, mostly developed countries, invest in non-Annex 1 parties, mostly less-developed nations. The investor from an Annex 1 party introduces advanced and efficient technologies into a host country. In return, the investor's country receives some part of the certified emissions reductions (CERs) generated by the project.[32] Parties that acquired CERs can increase their emissions by the same amount. The CDM itself will not increase or decrease the total amount of emissions in the world. However, the CDM projects must reduce emissions below the level that would have occurred in the absence of the CDM project activity.[33]

The CDM embodies the commitment established in the UN Framework Convention on Climate Change (FCCC) in May 1992 to "enable economic development to proceed in a sustainable manner." When developed country parties' energy technology would be made more efficient only at great cost, a project in another country would result in lower emissions into the global atmospheric commons, and technology transfer should help the host country to adjust the course of development in a manner less producing of emissions. The Kyoto Protocol stipulates that Annex 1 parties are to refrain from using CERs generated through nuclear facilities to meet their emission targets.[34]

Examples of certified CDM projects include a wind power plant project in the Patagonia region of Argentina involving Japan; a landfill gas capture and power generation project in Brazil involving the United Kingdom of Great Britain and Northern Ireland; a cogeneration project in Brazil involving Sweden; a biomass power plant, phases 1 and 2, in Chile, involving Japan and the United Kingdom; a wind power project in China involving the Netherlands; another wind power project in China involving Spain; another wind farm project in China involving Japan; a coal mine methane utilization and destruction project in China involving Switzerland; a hydropower project in China involving Italy; a wind power project in Ecuador involving Germany; a brick factory GHG reduction project in Egypt involving Canada and the Netherlands; several small hydroelectric projects in Honduras involving Finland; a waste heat captive power project in India involving the United Kingdom; the generation of electricity from windmills by Sun-n-Sand Hotels in India involving Germany; twenty-eight methane recovery and electricity generation projects in Mexico involving Switzerland and the United Kingdom; and a hydropower station regeneration project in Vietnam involving Japan. These illustrate the kind of "Energy industries, renewable and nonrenewable" projects certified. Other projects focus on energy distribution, energy demand, manufacturing industries, and chemical industries. While the large number of host countries (46) consenting to or welcoming CDM projects is worth noting, also remarkable are the numbers of CDM projects involving energy industries, the largest category of projects by far, hosted by Brazil (83), China (119), India (241), and Mexico (40), and the dearth of projects hosted by African nations.[35] Yet one of the purposes of the Clean Development Mechanism is to assist developing country host parties to achieve sustainable development in a manner consistent with the purposes of the UN Framework Convention on Climate Change. Africa is the region with the lowest per capita consumption. Incentives to invest in Africa are low compared to incentives to invest in other regions.

It is not uncommon for developing nations to be more concerned about increasing per capita wealth and decreasing local and regional pollution (brown emissions), than decreasing GHG emissions (green emissions). The CDM projects usually decrease both "brown" and "green" emissions.

Representatives of nations deliberating about the treaty that will follow the Kyoto Treaty after its commitment period (2008–12) have experience with these three market mechanisms and have the opportunity to correct for their weaknesses. Some of the successes and failures of these mechanisms are already known and provide good reasons for moral deliberation. The next chapter will go into more depth about the moral issues such treaty making occasions.

CHAPTER TWO

Moral Dimensions of Climate Change: Four Formulations

Calculations of consequences, considerations of fairness/justice, acceptance when appropriate of moral responsibility, the desire to act consistently with moral commitments, and the prioritizing of values are moral dimensions of climate change policy formulation that are explicit in the current public discussions, and I will shortly show how. Because the Conferences of the Parties, where these debates happen, are "so far away," and the scientific materials being generated are so voluminous, it may appear that the distance between policy and people is great. Yet more grassroots public discourse is absolutely necessary at this time, and desirable from the viewpoint of the Intergovernmental Panel on Climate Change (IPCC), because these policies are still being shaped, argued over, refined, and assessed. People who have been nurtured in faith communities have an opportunity to engage in public policy discernment through whatever practices of social witness their communities' polities encourage. This chapter will illustrate some ways of formulating the moral dimensions of climate change policy, and at this point I will use primarily public language, that is language that does not rely on special revelation for its knowledge. The next chapter will point down the road that takes us to using critically the resources of religious traditions to meet the moral challenges facing the global atmospheric commons.

The Consequences of Not Curtailing Emissions Will Be Catastrophic

It seems not to be a foregone conclusion that nations should take steps to lower their GHG (greenhouse gas) emissions. The United States, Canada, Russia, and China stand to gain some agricultural productivity if the climate warms. These nations' incentive structure is affected by their anticipation of greater food production, and in this sense they have perverse incentives. The United States, Canada, and Russia are also exporters of fossil-fuel energy, compounding the perversity.

Furthermore, the industrialized nations have systems to adapt to and cope with climate change: "factors such as wealth, technology, education, information, skills, infrastructure, access to resources, and management capabilities."[1] The least developed countries are generally poorer with regard to these factors, and consequently they have less capacity to adapt and are more vulnerable to climate-induced damage. The higher the level of warming, the higher the level of net losses to these developing countries. Developed nations, on the other hand, would experience a mix of gains and losses, the gains offsetting the losses and perhaps in some instances surpassing them, at least at the early stage. These gains are likely to be short-lived and counteracted by the more frequent damaging extreme events, such as hurricanes, floods, and heat waves.[2]

As a consequence, the current disparity between developed and developing countries in terms of levels of well-being will increase. The disparity grows the higher the mean temperature is projected.[3] Considering population distribution, with more population living in the developing countries, more people are projected to be harmed than benefited by climate change, even for small temperature increases.

The math in a utilitarian calculus leads to the conclusion that world bodies should adopt policies and measures that will slow and then reverse emissions of greenhouse gases. That is, to the question What makes a policy right? utilitarians answer, "those measures that, given the options available, will result in the greatest good and least harm for the greatest number." Such a utilitarian calculus takes seriously foreseeable consequences of climate change and weighs those against foreseeable consequences of slowing climate change and stabilizing the climate, calculating equally the well-being of each person who will be affected—and, to be thorough, also considering other species' well-being. The IPCC states with medium confidence that approximately 20 to 30 percent of species assessed so far are likely to be at increased risk of extinction if temperatures warm over 1.5 to 2.5 degrees Celsius relative to 1999 levels.[4] On utilitarian grounds, the release of GHGs should be curtailed significantly, to within the limits of the absorptive capacity of the atmosphere.

Gender Component of Consequential Analysis

Although climate change will affect men as well as women, an adequate consequential analysis of its effects will require a gender analysis, because the poor, the majority of whom are women living in developing countries, will suffer the greatest impact. In recognition of gender inequality's impact on women's well-being in the face of direct and indirect risks of a changing climate, December 2007 saw the establishment of the Global Gender and Climate Alliance at the Bali Conference of the Parties to the United Nations Framework Convention on Climate Change (UNFCCC). Among the purposes of the GGCA are to integrate a gender perspective into global policymaking, to ensure that UN financing addresses poor women and men equitably, and to bring women's voices into the policy discussions. Advocacy for women is needed at these levels in planning both mitigation and adaptation strategies.[5]

Mitigation of climate change phenomena refers to reduction of greenhouse gases in the atmosphere. Mitigation will occur mainly not through reduction of economic growth but through the substitution of new, cleaner technologies for carbon-based technologies. The Clean Development Mechanism supports mitigation projects that are supposed to have a development effect, but the pressure on sponsors to capitalize the carbon mitigation may have the effect of their favoring large-scale power, manufacturing, and forestry sink projects. Women may be involved in any of these projects as employees, and all would gain from increased access to electricity. Other kinds of projects, smaller and more dispersed, involving household energy, agriculture, and food processing, forest management, water pumping in rural areas, and energy appliances and processing in urban areas would make a big difference in a wide range of these daily responsibilities.[6] The CDM would certainly have room for such projects, but they may not be as attractive to carbon investors as the large investments in industry.[7]

Gender analysis is also needed in choosing adaptation measures, assistance with adaptation to the inevitable effects of the current enlarged concentration of greenhouse gases. Adaptation measures include civil engineering work to shore up dikes and seawalls, and projects in agriculture and forestry to enable populations to maintain their livelihoods in the face of climate change. Women have much at stake in these adaptation measures, and such measures should be approached in a gender-sensitive manner.[8]

Capacity building focused on women's needs will be necessary. One aspect of capacity building should be to assist women's groups to lobby for CDM adaptation projects that target women's particular vulnerabilities to climate change, such as the lack of alternative income possibilities, their greater dependence on the kinds of primary resources in agriculture and fisheries most threatened by climate change,[9] and their greater responsibility for the care of the increased numbers of the sick expected from higher levels of malaria, cholera, and heat stress.[10]

Gender-related vulnerability to climate change is closely related to the vulnerabilities of all poor in less-developed countries; women in developing countries experience high levels of pre-disaster poverty, often experiencing unequal status in the workforce, more likely employed in the informal sector and having less equitable access to land and other natural resources compared to men. This gender construction results in socially constructed vulnerability.[11]

The specific vulnerabilities of the poor and women within that strata will vary from region to region. West Africa, particularly the Sahel, has a propensity to drought and desertification, which will be exacerbated by climate change, threatening access to food security and safe water.[12] Bangladesh is subject to monsoon rains flooding about one-third of its land annually. The floods bring silt that fertilizes the fields, so when there is no flood, the fertility is diminished, reducing the yield. Fish breeding also depends on floods creating ponds and interconnections between waterways. The rural population distinguishes between good floods and bad floods, and the majority of the rural population would lose out rather than benefit from engineering measures such as embankments and river containment.[13] Climate change is anticipated to bring to Bangladesh rising sea levels and a retreating coastline, causing the loss of 18 percent of the country's land area, and the impact of cyclones deeper inland than is currently experienced. Women will become increasingly affected by intensified hazards, and cultural factors discouraging women from seeking shelter without shame or harassment will need to be addressed, as well as their vulnerability to poverty upon becoming widowed or divorced.[14]

The impact of the El Niño phenomenon on the rural upland communities of the Piura region of Peru provides another illustration of the likelihood that women will be affected distinctively by the climate change phenomena. El Niño is becoming more severe and is expected to accelerate. The storms during 1997–98 exemplified the way heavy rainfall causing soil, forest, and crop degradation, is leading to decreased agricultural production for small-scale farmers. The national agrarian policy has no focus on small-scale agriculture. As a consequence, food insecurity, rural to urban migration of men, and pressure on woods to supplement agriculture has increased.

In this context, limited access to education, specialist technical assistance, health care, or control over the family's productive resources for women has made them particularly vulnerable to food insecurity and malnutrition during El Niño. Although men have increased their migration out of the area and into coastal valleys, the major rural community organizations, largely led by men, did not recognize women as heads of households. The formation of women's survival organizations provided opportunities for women to demonstrate their skills as community leaders. Yet men held all the technical, management, and decision-making roles in the principal organization charged with responding to the disaster. Women, as it developed, were burdened with extra tasks in coping with the storm's effects, with no political or social recognition or power.[15]

In sum, the effects of climate change will be different in different regions and will make the already vulnerable more vulnerable, necessitating sensitivity to the distinctive impacts on the poor, among whom are women in disproportionate numbers. Adaptation measures are necessary to help the large number of people who have in the past and will increasingly face a threat to their livelihood and well-being. These measures will not substitute for mitigation, but neither can they be ignored.

Assessing Kyoto Policies' Ecological Effectiveness

Even granting the validity of consequential calculations to determine the morality of policies, it might be argued that the Kyoto process has not created the policies that should be implemented. I will not take this stance for reasons that will become evident in the next two sections, but I take this reservation very seriously: Because the scale of the climate issue is global, all of the world's major emitting nations must eventually participate in commitments to reduce emissions. The Kyoto process is designed to phase in commitments over time in two ways. First, the stringency of the commitments are initially rather low and will need to be revised upward over time. Second, the treaty was designed to be implemented even in the absence of full participation of all the major GHG emitters, with the idea that participation will broaden over time to include more developed, in transition, and developing nations. Thus, the Kyoto policies have incorporated "sequencing" of degrees of stringency and sequencing of breadth of participation. Nevertheless, the policies are designed so that early actions will make an effective contribution to the problem, should make subsequent expansion possible, and should not lock in an ineffective policy.[16] The fact that the treaty has a very specific "commitment period," which can open up to revisions for the following commitment period, is the main avenue for sequencing on these two fronts.

Is sequencing effective? If all major nations involved in GHG emitting do not undertake simultaneous mitigation commitments from the outset, the consequences are concerning. The provisions of the Framework Convention support initial mitigation efforts by the rich industrialized countries, with the developing countries beginning mitigation efforts later. Both sequencing of degrees of stringency and sequencing of breadth of participation are embedded in the principle to which the treaty appeals—"common but differentiated responsibility." This principle means that all nations have an obligation to address the climate issue, but not in the same way or at the same time. In particular, according to UNFCCC Article 3.1, "the developed-country Parties should take the lead in combatting climate change and the adverse effects thereof."[17]

But it is difficult to ignore the possibility that emission-intensive industries will escape emission controls by relocating to countries that have not accepted commitments, thus increasing the incentive for those countries to delay taking on commitments. Emissions will move abroad rather than being reduced. Then, if an effort is mounted to expand the Kyoto regime, it will be more expensive for the late joiners to buy in. Nevertheless, this concern is an argument based on consequences, anticipating the likelihood that firms will delay the expense of effective technological upgrades as long as foreign investment makes it possible to delay.

It is not possible to learn how the global climate is changing without being concerned about the consequences of continuing along the path of business as usual for ourselves and our children and other species of animals and plants. It will be, because it already is, calamitous. Assuming some consensus, then, that global warming should be effectively slowed and curtailed, what are other moral considerations relevant to choosing the mechanisms for doing so? If implementation of change is to have wide support, such implementations will have to be considered fair. Serious questions about fairness are definitely affecting international relations.

It Is Not Obvious That Choosing 1990 as the Base Year for Assigning Emission Allowances Is Fair

Having reached the position that emissions-reducing policies are warranted on consequentialist grounds, the choice of which policies to adopt involves determining which are fair, in addition to having a likelihood of success. An *intragenerational* dimension to concerns about "fairness" is involved when countries enjoying a rich lifestyle emit substantial quantities of GHGs into the atmosphere without paying those countries that are not emitting as much. Not paying a fair price for such dumping is a form of exploitation of neighbors across borders, and exploitation is by definition wrong. In addition, the current and past generations are liable to charges of *intergenerational* exploitation, as CO_2 and other gases have been released into the atmosphere since industrialization. Their cumulative effect is being compounded for future generations, who are not here to argue their case, thus putting us in the position of having to consider their interests.[18]

The question of how to address both the intragenerational and the intergenerational dimensions of unfair use of the atmosphere is what is at stake in the dissension about choosing 1990 as the base year for assigning emission allowances.

The current allocation of "assigned amounts" of emission allowances follows the so-called grandfathering rule, such that emission allowances are derived from historic emission levels. Parties that have produced the greatest amount of GHGs are assigned more emission allowances. Industrialized countries, responsible for emitting 80 percent of GHGs since 1800, have claimed the right to pollute based on having polluted first, and ignoring the question of whether access to greenhouse gas–emitting world resources in the past has been just.[19] The other proposed basis for distributing emission allowances would be equality, such that nations would be assigned allowances based on their population level at a negotiated date.[20]

The point of view that emission rights should be based on *equal* per capita access to clean air was represented at the Kyoto meeting and continues to be present during the negotiation sessions. A consistent voice for this view is that of the Centre for Science and Environment in New Delhi, India.

> Reducing carbon dioxide emissions from human activities has high costs. In all fairness, most of these costs should be met by countries that have contributed the most to the problem, while providing a space to grow for people of those nations who have contributed little. The costs and benefits of the management of the atmosphere, a global common property resource, have to be shared equitably among all human beings. And the best way to do this would be to decide per capita entitlements to the atmosphere.[21]

Disagreement over the basis for emission allowances is not a disagreement about whether to use markets in emissions as a way of controlling global warming. People who urge a per capita basis for determining responsibilities and obligations may well advocate market instruments.[22] But if the base year is 1800 rather than 1990, rights to use clean atmosphere are effectively distributed on a per capita basis rather than a per country basis, because emissions from industrialization did not begin to affect the atmosphere until about 1800.

Nor is this disagreement about whether emissions *trading* should be included in climate change policy. Before the Framework Convention, the Global Commons Institute in the United Kingdom presented a proposal using contraction (to a level of global GHG emissions) and convergence (so that each country converges on the same allocation per inhabitant by an agreed date), aimed at equality in emissions per capita. In this proposal, countries unable to manage within their shares would be able to buy the unused parts of the allocations of other countries.[23]

The disagreement is not even about whether developing countries should have obligations to *limit* their emissions, as opposed to reducing emissions. It is true that developing nations express resentment when pressured to limit emissions while industrialized nations (with the exception of the European Union) are not providing leadership in reducing their emissions. Limits on emissions in developing countries are perceived as limits to growth, and they also imply consolidation at current levels of emissions per capita.[24] However, poor nations will suffer most from climate change, and they have less ability to adapt to such change. So they have a stake in lowering global GHG emissions. It is frequently representatives from NGOs (nongovernmental organizations) in the developing nations who insist that ecological effectiveness is as important as equity in atmospheric management policies. Strong voices from southern nations call for a carbon-free economy as the preferable path to development.[25] If developing nations continue along the carbon path that industrialized nations have taken, developing nations' emissions will certainly equal and then surpass industrialized nations' by the year 2030.

The conflict centers on developing nations' perceptions that current targets to lower GHG emissions use 1990 actual emissions as the standard for establishing obligations for the first commitment period, 2008–12. If obligations in future commitment periods are emendations of these obligations, in combination with the three flexibility mechanisms, they fear that status-quo relationships among industrialized and developing countries will be maintained. Such relationships lack equal rights to use the atmospheric commons.

> Developing countries see this as a way of freezing global inequity. All nations have an equal right to the absorptive capacity of the atmosphere, a global common. Industrialized countries have already used up more than their share, having embarked on the path to development long before developing countries. Developing countries want clear entitlements based on per capita emissions of GHGs before any emissions trading is allowed under the North-South mechanism, the CDM (the Clean Development Mechanism).[26]

Such entitlements would be allocated to countries on the basis of population size.[27]

Proposals calling for contraction and convergence represent a way to implement per capita equality in the long run. Industrialized countries have nearly locked themselves into a fossil-based infrastructure that requires some lead time to dismantle, even disregarding resistance from power and oil companies. Factors other than population size need to be taken into account, including geographical and climatic conditions, and intensity of the economy. Contraction in carbon emissions is nevertheless a path for industrialized nations to start down.[28] For contraction and convergence policies to be implemented, nations would need to agree to stay within safe limits of the climate system. A scientifically derived global carbon budget would be the upper limit for all combined emissions, and that budget would be divided among the countries of the world. Industrialized nations would start the contraction process with more of this global budget but would receive fewer and fewer allowances as time goes on. Industrializing nations would begin at a point of much lower levels of emissions but would in the process of development increase those emissions, receiving a larger share of the emissions budget. While the polluting nations would engage in a process of contraction, the developing nations would eventually converge with the industrialized nations at a point that is safely within the absorptive capacity of the atmosphere. That point could represent per capita global equality.

On the whole, however, the question of justice in the distribution of emission allowances is missing from the discussion of the Kyoto Protocol by representatives of what are sometimes called the "umbrella" nations, including Japan, Canada, Australia, and the United States.[29] To them it does not matter where emissions originate, because wherever they originate they affect the whole atmosphere. It is more cost effective to lower emissions in poor nations than in industrialized nations, so the first efforts should focus on emissions in poor nations, concerns about harvesting "the low-hanging fruit" notwithstanding.[30]

Of course, the documents from the 1992 Framework Convention on Climate Change, which contain the objectives, may have set up this conflict. In them, the purpose of the Kyoto Protocol is to stabilize GHG concentrations in the atmosphere at a level that would prevent dangerous anthropogenic interference with the climate system. The objective contains no explicit mandate to seek justice in the implementation of climate policies to effect this end. The treaties governing use of the atmosphere have abundantly called for equity in designing such measures. But *equity* by definition represents the compromise reached when different views of justice are in conflict, and representatives of NGOs and some southern nations are suspicious of this term.

In the context of the particular conflict before us, the word *equity* communicates a desire to dodge the question of whether each person in the world has an equal right to clean air, a global commons. Raul A. Estrada-Oyuela, who chaired the Kyoto meeting, commented on the use of the word *equity*:

We know that all human beings are born equal, with the same rights and duties. However, we clearly realize that in these global environmental matters, neither human beings nor nations are equal, and consequently we talk about equity instead of talking about equality.

It was different before; at least it was different in the words we used. Principle I of the Declaration on the Human Environment adopted at Stockholm in 1972 proclaims the equality of human beings, but principle 3 of the Rio Declaration on Environment and Development says that "the right to development must be fulfilled so as to equitably meet developmental and environmental needs of the present and future generations."[31]

The appeal to equity is a compromise principle. It takes seriously the gap between where the nations are and where we would need to go to be fair. Fairness language and justice language are near equivalents, and both signal a kind of moral reasoning that determines what is right by assessing the intrinsic moral logic of claims (deontology). What is right is intrinsically right making, not determined by accounting of "goods" alone, though consideration of consequences may be involved. What is wrong is intrinsically wrong making, regardless of good consequences that might be anticipated. Fairness is inherently right; exploitation is inherently wrong. Fairness should be a mark of public policy, and fairness trumps other kinds of considerations that are based on preferences or convenience. In addition, people will not change their consumption and production habits on a consistent basis unless they believe it is fair to do so. So fairness has political leverage.

Forward Movement Is Possible Only When Nations Stop Jockeying over "Responsibility"

The conflict over what justice and equity mean and require continues to undermine the negotiations and implementation of climate policies. The deep conflict in North–South relations is a big component in the reluctance of sovereign nations to adopt effective climate policies. The world's eyes are on China, India, Brazil, and Indonesia, because these nations are rapidly developing. But the anger and mistrust are not limited to these countries, whose economies are in transition. The anger and mistrust have several aspects:

There is a vast difference in responsibility for the problem of climate change. The richest 20 percent of the world's population is responsible for over 60 percent of current greenhouse gas emissions. If you take the historical view, rich nations are responsible for 80 percent of GHGs, and the historical view is appropriate because CO_2 remains in the atmosphere for more than one hundred years and perhaps as long as two hundred years.

A complicating factor is that poor nations may have very polluting elites who control a large share of their nations' productive capital and live international jet-dependent lifestyles. They maintain their hold on their wealth through abrogation of human rights, particularly labor and environmental rights. Moreover, they may block development strategies that involve broadening their nations' economic base. Similarly in the North we have two-thirds world populations who do not benefit from the growing GDP (Gross Domestic Product) because of the loss of unionization, defunding of social programs, and militarization, causing the polarization of wealth and poverty in the United States in particular. So the North–South conflict should not be depicted in overly simplistic terms.

While the responsibility for GHGs lies overwhelmingly in the northern use of fossil fuels, the *impact* of climate change will fall very heavily on the southern nations, who are least able to protect their citizens from vulnerability.

> [T]heir populations are larger, their economies are more vulnerable to the climate, and they are far less able to afford the measures that would be needed to mitigate climate change, such as sea walls, changes in agricultural practices, or even wider use of air conditioning.[32]

Developing countries will be the principal beneficiaries of climate change policy. Yet the dynamics of negotiations replicate the uneven power dynamic that makes southern nations poor to begin with, from their perspective.

Southern nations tend to assume a development strategy that mimics the strategy rich nations took: reliance on earnings from carbon-intensive export products, including input-intensive agriculture and manufacturing. Because developed nations have to some degree shifted manufacturing off-shore, through economic globalization, and because poorer nations such as China are relying on carbon-intensive manufacturing for raising incomes domestically, they are reluctant to discuss *limits* on GHGs at this point. The IPCC's Fourth Assessment Report of Working Group II in effect said the world can avoid the catastrophic consequences of global warming by using biofuels and renewable energy. China's negotiators repeatedly try to tone down some elements of draft texts to remove scenarios it fears would affect its short-term growth.[33]

The United States and other umbrella nations refuse to accept responsibility for their role as the largest GHG emitter, which some nations find particularly galling. China and India try to put the responsibility for global warming on North America and Europe and also the responsibility for solving the climate change problem. But the United States particularly holds such claims to be solely negotiating strategies and dismisses them out of hand.

Moral responsibility belongs to those who cause something to happen, knowingly and willingly; or, after learning of the negative effects of policies, refuse to correct for them. Persons or nations are excused from all or degrees of responsibility when their actions are limited by lack of information or lack of capacity to do something different.

The industrialized nations' economic patterns of production and consumption since 1800 are the source of most greenhouse gas emissions. We know this. Our policy-makers continue to favor policies that have, as a result, these harms, knowingly and willingly. Industrialized nations know how to decrease GHGs, and some are doing it. But the United States, responsible for 22 percent, persists in using a pattern of economic development that relies heavily on the availability of low-price fossil energy, and, with some neighbors, avoids the measures that would internalize harms to the atmosphere in the price of the goods and services produced with carbon-based fuels. Persisting in this pattern of short-term calculation of economic development, with the knowledge that there are alternative energy policies available, makes such industrialized countries morally responsible for harming the global atmospheric commons.

The citizens of developed countries have a role to play in forcing the laggard nations to accept responsibility for harms we continue to perpetrate. The "character" of our peoples, as perceived by other peoples and by ourselves, is at stake. If citizens of industrialized nations allow representative negotiators to claim in effect, "We know we have a large impact on the global atmospheric commons, but we do not want to be inconvenienced by having to pay the true price of the energy and transport we use—*plus* you can't make us," then who are we as peoples of this realm? The term "bullies" comes to mind. It costs too much social capital to be perceived as bullies and to perceive ourselves as bullies. Bullies are by definition immoral, devoid of character or virtue.

Moral Responsibility Is Relevant
for Achieving Justice

The desire for justice by the southern nations is much deeper than a negotiating strategy. They have a worldview in which they are victimized by unequal power dynamics in international trade rooted in colonialism and the extension of economic dependency after becoming politically independent. Southern nations are very sensitive to global inequality. The colonial impact on deskilling of indigenous leaders and focus on one or two resources for export have had long-term consequences affecting southern nations' vulnerability to climate change today. Unstable commodity prices, declining terms of trade, domestic political unrest, high levels of social inequality, and feeble postcolonial political institutions constitute structural barriers to southern development.[34]

These barriers are in part fed by internal domestic dynamics. But the southern nations' perception that their vulnerability to climate disasters is tied to economic and political weakness is reality-based. According to Timmons Roberts and Bradley Parks, the World Bank, UNDP (United Nations Development Programme), and the International Federation of Red Cross and Red Crescent organizations report that 90 percent of disaster victims live in developing countries, and 97 percent of all disaster-related deaths occur in the developing world. But their research calls into question the simple assumption that *poverty* is the primary determinant of human vulnerability to natural disasters. They found that it is not poverty per se but a suite of variables that can be traced back to a common causal origin: dependence on a narrow range of low-value exports. Nations whose participation in international trade is limited to such low-value exports (such as mining and logging as well as ranching and plantation agriculture) tend to have a colonial past, a small elite that controls the exports, low levels of government spending on social programs, ill-defined property rights, and disregard for development benefiting the base of the population. They further found that national wealth is less important than freedom of the press, property rights, and curbs on income inequality in the ability of people to be resilient to hydro-meteorological disasters.[35]

Therefore international and domestic efforts, including church-based efforts, to protect human rights may have a positive influence on nations' capacities to reduce citizens' vulnerability to disasters. This is because human rights make a space for people to pressure their governments.

The reluctance of the umbrella nations to address seriously their obligation to create economic relations of parity is responsible for southern nations' mistrust of climate negotiations. However, most future emissions growth will probably come from today's developing countries. Their populations are growing rapidly, as is their share of energy-intensive industries.

Between 2004 and 2030, developing nations are likely to account for over three-quarters of the increase in energy-related CO_2 emissions, with China accounting for over one-third of the increase.[36] Yet the southern nations also play a role in blocking possibilities for ecological policies. A few southern perceptions that obstruct North–South relations in dealing with climate are these:

- Climate change is primarily an issue of profligate northern consumption.
- A nation's ability to implement meaningful environmental reform depends on its position in the international division of labor.
- The North is using environmental issues as a ruse to thwart economic development of poor nations.[37]

The capacity to achieve international agreements on the climate is being blocked by perceptions on the part of the South that the institutions responsible for facilitating the agreements are fundamentally unjust and that the deliberations to date have failed to take the justice issues seriously. This sense of injustice is exacerbated when wealthy nations show disdain for the Kyoto Treaty. Secretary of State Madeleine Albright, in her statement before the International Relations Committee in February 1998, said, "Kyoto . . . made a significant down payment on securing the meaningful participation of developing countries in the needed global response [to lower greenhouse gas emissions], but clearly more must be done to meet our requirements."[38] On February 14, 2002, President George W. Bush stated at the Science Center of the National Oceanic and Atmospheric Administration: "As president of the United States, charged with safeguarding the welfare of the American people and American workers, I will not commit our nation to an unsound international treaty that will throw millions of our citizens out of work." Never mind what justice might require by virtue of U.S. responsibility for greenhouse gases.

But the tendency to duck the question of what is just finds a home also in public policy literature authored in the United States.

> A realistic climate policy cannot rely on large international transfers to prevent individual countries from being made worse off. In the language of game theory, participation in a climate change agreement must be incentive-compatible for each country.
>
> Unfortunately, much of the debate over the distributional aspects of climate change policy has focused on a different and far less practical question: *which countries are ethically responsible for reducing climate change?* Some observers argue that industrialized countries are obligated to do the most to avoid climate change because they have generated most of the greenhouse gases now in the atmosphere. Others argue that developing countries account for a large and growing share of emissions and that no climate policy will succeed without significant participation by the developing world. There is some truth in both of these positions, *but neither is a realistic way to approach designing a policy that will have to be ratified by sovereign nations.* Instead, the focus must be on developing a pragmatic policy that will allow all countries to make a firm commitment to cut emissions over time.[39]

These authors believe that it is not "useful" to establish what fairness or justice requires. But what may also be in play is that poor nations and rich nations hold almost diametrically opposed views of justice.

As I mentioned earlier, the operative theory of justice in existing climate agreements is "grandfathering," such that emission allowances are derived from historic emission levels. Parties that have produced the greatest amount of GHGs are assigned more emission allowances. Industrialized countries have claimed the right to pollute based on having polluted first, ignoring the question of whether access to world resources in the past has been just.[40]

A second theory of justice is based on "equal rights of the world's citizens to the atmospheric global commons." Choosing a base year for population levels of the different countries, perhaps 1990, this theory submits that every human on Earth has equal rights to the global atmosphere, and therefore allocations of how much each can pollute should be done on a per capita basis.[41]

A third theory of justice is based on "historical responsibility." Brazilian negotiators have been the most articulate that a country's greenhouse gas reductions should depend on its relative contribution to the global temperature rise. This perspective criticizes all theories of justice based on current emissions, since the concentration of GHGs has taken years to build up, through the process of industrialization in the northern countries. Since virtually all the CO_2 emitted since 1945 is still in the atmosphere, rich nations would be required to make deep and immediate cuts. By 2010, Britain would have to reduce its emissions by 66 percent, the United States by 23 percent, and Japan by 8 percent.[42]

Finally, George W. Bush promoted a theory of justice by which the standard is "lower carbon intensity" per dollar of GDP. He committed America to an aggressive new strategy to cut greenhouse gas intensity by 18 percent over the next ten years.[43] Lowering intensity does not lower actual concentrations of greenhouse gases. Rather, it accommodates economic growth. It represents the notion that some people see this theory as one of justice, but it takes a wide imagination to see how.

Theories of justice by grandfathering and by lowering carbon intensity are represented by negotiators from the United States, Canada, and Australia. Theories of justice by equality and historical responsibility have been offered by negotiators from the rapidly developing countries.[44]

The political logjam we have witnessed takes the form of a few industrialized nations, particularly the nation from which I come, refusing to commit to lower emissions until developing countries commit, and developing countries refusing to commit owing to the historical responsibility of industrialized nations for spoiling the air in the first place. Policy from here on out should be driven by the principles well acknowledged by the Framework Convention, including common but differentiated responsibility and ecological effectiveness. The former principle obligates industrialized nations to take leadership in technology and in policy to lower emissions. The second principle requires developing nations to agree to accept commitments in the future, during the treaty's new commitment periods, the negotiations for which are designed to consider new data on the effects of emissions on climate change and the speed with which it is occurring. The language used to refer to the issues these principles address is fluid. In the Fourth Assessment Report, Working Group III says a successful agreement about how to fulfill the treaty will have to be environmentally effective and cost-effective, will have to incorporate distributional considerations and equity, and will have to be institutionally feasible.[45] Perhaps this language is more functional than the earlier way of formulating the principles.

The Kyoto Treaty's mechanisms are also designed to accept new members, to provide incentives for them to join, and to make emission decreases more stringent. In this respect the treaty's mechanisms are worth supporting. However, the effort to lower carbon intensity alone does not conform with the principle of ecological effectiveness.

Another approach that resonates with "common but differentiated responsibility" and "ecological effectiveness" claims that distributive justice is linked to restorative justice, because *distributive justice and restorative justice are intrinsically related.* Restorative justice is necessary when a breach in relationships has been caused and the relationship needs repair. Often associated with criminal justice, restorative justice puts offenders in direct relationship with those they have harmed for the purpose of creating a new relationship, allowing both the offender and harmed to redefine their roles in relationship to each other and past wrongs. It requires people to deal with responsibility and liability and may allow both the offender and the offended to become moral agents in a mature way. "Restore" can refer to healing a broken relationship, and it can also refer to repairing natural systems.

When Annex 1 countries (or developed countries more generally) enter into CDM projects, they enter as countries with histories that affect their current political and economic standing in relationship to each other. If a less-developed country has a history of colonialism, it may feel the urgency of "brown objectives" more than the "green objectives" that will decrease GHGs. So the scope of the CDM should include not only "green objectives," attentive to avoiding CO_2 emissions, but also "brown objectives," of concern to poor nations but not necessarily effective in lowering GHGs, such as infrastructure for clean water, sewage, clean air, and landfill—projects that decrease the effect of pollution on the quality of life of the base of the population. Including "brown objectives" in the CDM can be a component of restorative justice.

When developing the "green objectives," in addition, several NGOs have proposed limiting the projects to renewable energy, off the carbon path (not coal, oil, or nuclear). And the projects should be manageable domestically without dependence on outside talent. Supporting poor nations' development off the carbon path may be the most productive approach to linking distributive and restorative justice. Such projects will encourage long-term renewable energy technology for all countries. They will not substitute cost-effectiveness for ecological effectiveness. And to enter such projects will likely sidestep the carbon fuel industry as it exists, stimulating new technology.

The writers of the Fourth Assessment Report (2007) estimated 2,400 GW (gigawatts) of new power plants will be required by 2030 in developing countries to supply their energy services, now supplied mainly by fossil fuels. An investment of five trillion U.S. dollars will be required to deliver these power plants, and this situation presents an opportunity for sustainable development. If this development opportunity can be linked to GHG mitigation, the development path will result in a more secure energy supply than imported energy can provide, technological innovation, air-pollution abatement, and employment at the local level. The writers acknowledge that while electricity, transport fuels, and heat supplied by renewable energy are less prone to price fluctuations, in many cases they may have higher costs. In addition, the investment costs of new energy system infrastructures can be a barrier to their implementation. But since "renewable energy technologies can be more labour intensive than conventional technologies per unit of energy output, more employment will result."[46] Investment in renewable energy, if it is appropriate to the local and regional context, is one significant approach to linking distributive and restorative justice. As a consequence, it is possible to claim that generation of wealth is not the first measure of a good economy. The measure of an economy should be its capacity to ensure the health of the people, flora, and fauna in the community and of the community itself. Thus, we see the significance of taking seriously the context in which parties to the negotiations are situated and of responding to real needs of the people and the ecologies they represent.

Summary

To become immersed in moral reflection on climate policies requires every significant mode of moral discourse, by which I mean efforts to discern the right require calculating consequences, acknowledging duties and obligations, accepting responsibility if appropriate, reflecting on the character of who we are as individuals and as peoples, and considering the global context: these forms of discourse are all in play and necessary. To deal seriously with any one moral dimension propels one inevitably to the next and then the next moral dimension. Not to detract from the legitimacy of national governance, but to be citizens of nations and states, we now also must accept the obligations of Earth citizenship, and national sovereignty must be accountable to the treatment of the global atmospheric commons. Earth citizenship involves using every mode of moral discourse, responding to the demands of our own ecological context and allowing others to respond to their particular contexts. In the meantime, each strategy that is chosen to respond to the spoiling of the global atmospheric commons must measure the parts per million of CO_2 that accumulates in our air envelope. Different nations' obligations are affected by their historical contexts, but the climate system responds to all of us as an undifferentiated collectivity, no matter where the gases come from.

In the next chapter I pose one further method of identifying the moral dimensions of climate change policy. It involves choosing the vision that will shape our and our grandchildren's and their grandchildren's futures.

CHAPTER THREE

Choosing Our Future:
A Fifth Formulation

Which Future Should We Value?

The debates about consequences, what is fair, what responsibility for the historical situation engenders, and what justice requires can be engaged using the language of the public square. But when it comes to this fifth dimension, choosing a future and living intentionally into it, we may feel compelled to employ religious language or be explicit about religious commitments. For instance, the World Council of Churches, as a body, has observer status at the Conference of the Parties meetings, giving voice to Christian communities, churches, and agencies. Its spokespersons have consistently urged the parties to adopt practices based on principles of justice, equity, solidarity, human development, and environmental conservation. Using the language of faith, the WCC spokespersons confess that we believe that "the earth was entrusted to us but we simply cannot do whatever we want with it. We cannot make use of nature using it only as a commodity. We must bear in mind that our liberty does not allow us to destroy that which sustains life on our planet."[1] This faithful witness has been present consistently at the meetings. Traveling in the tracks they have left in the snow and mud, I want to propose that religious commitments or the lack thereof may be functioning in the climate change discussions, affecting the vision of the future we advocate now.

Scientists of the IPCC (remember that they provide data about the economic and social dimensions of climate change as well as the scientific-technical analyses of impacts) have devised a method for making available the range of possible directions policy might take and their probable impacts on the natural, social, and economic environments. These scientists have proposed four scenarios that can be narrated using "story lines," each representing a possible future. Each story line takes a different direction, forging a path that, as we go down it, becomes increasingly but not totally irreversible. They view all scenarios as equally possible, and they introduce no assumptions as to which is "central," nor do they rely on surprises or disasters. What is very important, they exclude references to policies for greenhouse gas mitigation in the scenarios. That is, no scenario assumes implementation of the United Nations Framework Convention for Climate Change (UNFCCC) or the emissions targets in the Kyoto Protocol.[2]

The scenarios are imaged as four different areas of the crown of a tree, with all its branches and leaves. The trunk of the tree is the environment. The roots of the tree are the "driving forces": population prospects; economic development; energy intensities, energy demand, and the structure of energy use; technological change; and agriculture and its effect on land use change. On one side of the tree's crown are the two scenarios (A1 and A2) that emphasize sustained economic growth, one global and one regional, and anticipate sensitivity to environmental concerns to gain currency as affluence is achieved, if at all. On the other side of the crown are the two scenarios (B1 and B2) that emphasize economic growth within the framework of a commitment to environmental sustainability, one using global mechanisms and trade, the other using local and regional adaptations.[3] You may think of this conceptual arrangement as the IPCC Scenario Tree.

These four scenarios are played out for one hundred years, with different paradigms of social, economic, technological, and environmental relationships. Each will be viewed positively by some people and negatively by others. The Special Report on Emissions Scenarios (SRES) writing team, those responsible for developing the Special Report on Emissions Scenarios, had the material to develop thirty-five different story lines but chose to group them within the four main ones to avoid complicating the process with too many alternatives, which is why they are referred to as "families" of scenarios. While they do not include specific climate change policies, they do include other socioeconomic developments and nonclimate environmental policies. Each story line describes its effect on the amount of greenhouse gas emissions.[4]

Two aspects of this image of the Scenario Tree are remarkable. The first is that these IPCC scientists are able to show that it is futile to consider the "environment" in the absence of attention to population, economy, energy, technology, and agriculture. Proposals to protect the whole ecosystem and help it to flourish must take the form of proposals about all these driving forces. Such a comprehensive perspective is a positive model for all of us.

Second, these scientists did not view religious and cultural values as relevant enough to be considered a driving force. At the same time, they acknowledge that each scenario reflects a complex of priorities and institutional patterns that embody commitments to certain values, virtues, practices, and ends. Of course these values, virtues, practices, and ends are going to be influenced by religious and cultural commitments. Are they embedded in and indistinguishable from population, economy, technology, energy, and land use practices? Or do the scientists not have enough of a handle on the world's religious traditions to be able to factor them into the possible scenarios?

Or, perhaps, religion is thought to be private and unrelated to social policy, and therefore outside the scope of the IPCC mandate? All may be correct. I suspect, however, that the "religious factor" will never become irrelevant to the collective use of the atmospheric commons.

Finally, the Fourth Assessment Report indicates that, by 2007, the time of publication, the driving forces and emissions had not changed very much. Birth rates in many parts of the world have fallen more sharply than anticipated by the scenarios. But where they did, such lower population has been offset by higher rates of economic growth, and/or a shift to more carbon-intensive energy systems, such as a shift to coal because of increasing oil and gas prices.[5]

The four scenarios or story lines are useful here because they provide an opportunity to ask ourselves what we most value and why. Each story line requires a basket of policies, so along with each scenario goes opportunities for political direction. More interestingly, if the Council of All Beings[6] were to invite you to speak for the scenario you will support, and give reasons, your response will declare what you perceive to be "a good life." That description of the good life is another dimension of doing ethics, and in it you will disclose whether there will be room for the other council members and their kind by 2100.

I reproduce below each scenario for future world development from the IPCC "Special Report on Emissions Scenarios."[7] Because the SRES did not track the consequences of each scenario for ecosystem change, particularly with respect to biodiversity, I add material to the description of each scenario from the Millennium Ecosystem Assessment (MA) carried out between 2001 and 2005.[8] Together, these scenarios represent best guesses about how the nations of the world will develop using different policies or strategies, such as:

- economic policy reforms, such as reducing subsidies and internalizing into the price of goods "externalities," including pollution and emissions;

- strategies that emphasize local and regional safety and protection that give less emphasis to cross-border and global issues;
- strategies that emphasize the development and use of technologies allowing greater economic efficiency and adaptive control;
- strategies that emphasize adaptive management and local learning about the consequences of management interventions for ecosystem services.[9]

Two of the scenarios that follow escalate the present trend toward globalization and international cultural and economic connectedness. Two represent a less connected and more regional focus.

A1 Story Line and Scenario Family

The A1 story line is a case of *rapid and successful economic development*, in which regional average income per capita converges with other regions. Current distinctions between "poor" and "rich" countries eventually dissolve. The primary dynamics are:

- Strong commitment to market-based solutions
- High savings and commitment to education at the household level
- High rates of investment and innovation in education, technology, and institutions at the national and international levels
- International mobility of people, ideas, and technology[10]

The transition to economic convergence results from advances in transport and communication technology, shifts in national policies on immigration and education, and international cooperation in the development of national and international institutions that enhance productivity growth and technology diffusion.

In the A1 scenario family, demographic, and economic trends are closely linked, as affluence is correlated with long life and small families (low mortality and low fertility). Global population grows to some nine billion by 2050 and declines to seven billion by 2100. Gross Domestic Product (GDP) reaches US$550 trillion by 2100.

While the high average level of income per capita (US$21,000 by 2050) contributes to a great improvement in the overall health and social conditions of the majority of people, this world is not necessarily devoid of problems. In particular, many communities could face some of the problems of social exclusion encountered in the wealthiest countries during the twentieth century, and in many places income growth could produce increased pressure on the global commons.

Rapid technical progress results in reducing the resources needed to produce a given level of output. Energy use per unit of GDP decreases at an average annual rate of 1.3 percent. Environmental amenities are valued and rapid technological progress "frees" for other purposes natural resources currently devoted to provision of human needs. The current emphasis on "conservation" of nature gives way to active "management" of natural and environmental services, which increases ecologic resilience.

High incomes translate into increased consumption of meat and dairy products, increased car ownership, sprawling suburbia, and dense transport networks, nationally and internationally.

Some scenario groups in the A1 scenario family evolve along the carbon-intensive energy path consistent with the current development strategy of countries with abundant domestic coal resources. Fossil intensive development is designated (A1FI). A second scenario group sees dependence on non-fossil energy sources, meaning renewable energy and nuclear (A1T). A third group assumes a balanced mix of sources, with no single source predominant (A1B). The implications of these alternative development paths for future GHG emissions vary from the carbon-intensive (high emissions) to decarbonized paths (low emissions).

The Millennium Assessment Report version of the A1 scenario is called "Global Orchestration." This view of the future receives its impetus from the positive influence of globally orchestrated policy reforms. The emphasis of the reforms is on creating markets that allow equal participation of developing countries, providing them with equal access to goods and services. Global and regional standards for trade are enforced by such bodies as the World Trade Organization (WTO). In turn, faith in global institutions leads to strengthening of the United Nations.

As subsidies are removed, trade expands globally, and the demand for goods and services increases. A wealthier middle class develops in what are now less developed countries, and this class begins to demand cleaner cities, less pollution, and a more beautiful environment. Nevertheless, problems associated with intensified agriculture (uniform industrial methods and discount of local indigenous knowledge) and the slow loss of wildlands occur but are not given attention. Environmental problems difficult to address lead to biodiversity loss. In conjunction with agricultural specialization, which causes simplification of ecosystems, widespread trade has an unintended consequence of introduction of invasive species. Reduced diversity limits the options of ecosystems to respond to ecological surprises, including invasive species.[11]

The pattern demographers have noted in the past is that as people's incomes rise, some kinds of pollution start to fall and people place a higher value on environmental amenities. The A1 Global Orchestration scenario banks on this phenomenon. However, in the case of climate change, this hope is ill founded, in part because the demand for some carbon-intensive goods and services—air transport for one—will continue to increase as incomes rise. Breaking the link between income growth and emissions per person will occur only with policies triggering changes in preferences, relative prices of carbon-intensive goods, and breaks in technological trends.[12]

A2 Story Line and Scenario Family

The A2 scenario family represents a differentiated world. Compared to the A1 story line, it is characterized by less trade, relatively slow capital stock turnover, and slower technological change. The world consolidates into economic regions, and each region emphasizes self-reliance and less economic, social, and cultural interaction between regions. Economic growth is uneven, and the income gap between now-industrialized and developing parts of the world does not narrow.

People, ideas, and capital are less mobile, so that technology diffuses more slowly than in the other scenario families. International disparities in productivity and income per capita are either maintained or increased.

With the emphasis on family and community life, fertility rates decline slowly, which makes the population the largest among the story lines (fifteen billion by 2100). Global average per capita income is low relative to other story lines, reaching US$7,200 per capita by 2050 and US$16,000 in 2100. By 2100 the global GDP reaches about US$250 trillion.[13]

Technological change is more rapid than average in some regions and slower in others, because industry adjusts to local resource endowments, culture, and education levels. High-income but resource-poor regions shift toward advanced post-fossil technologies (renewables or nuclear), while low-income resource-rich regions generally rely on older fossil technologies. Final energy intensities in A2 decline with a pace of 0.5 to 0.7 percent per year. A combination of slow technological progress, more limited environmental concerns, and low land availability because of high population growth means that the energy needs of the A2 world are satisfied primarily by fossil (mostly coal) and nuclear energy. In some cases, however, regional energy shortages force investments into renewable alternatives.[14]

Social and political structures are also diversified. Some regions move toward stronger welfare systems and reduced income inequality, while others move toward "leaner" government and more heterogeneous income distributions. Because of high population, agricultural productivity is one of the main focus areas for innovation and research and development. Global environmental concerns are relatively weak, although attempts are made to bring regional and local pollution under control and to maintain environmental amenities.

Such a world could have many positive aspects from the current perspective, such as the increasing tendency toward cultural pluralism with mutual acceptance of diversity and fundamental differences.

The MA (Millennium Assessment Report) version of the A2 Scenario is named "Order from Strength," and is responsive to the effect of terrorism, war, and loss of trust in global institutions experienced at the beginning of the twenty-first century. Governments of the industrial nations focus inward, putting high value on national security, trade protectionism, and protecting borders. Religious fundamentalism reinforces this nationalism.

Environmental challenges are addressed only for purposes of securing resources for human consumption. Pockets of well-preserved wilderness in rich countries serve the purpose of holiday and leisure travel. Owing to the decrease of trade among countries, invasive species spread is checked.

Resource-intensive industries and food production are moved to poor countries to make rich nations' lands more livable. Poor people's environments experience degradation as a result, leading to widespread migrations from degraded areas.

Global issues such as climate change and international issues such as large river management are impossible to address as at least one key nation is unwilling to cooperate. Rich nations cooperate among themselves to address environmental concerns, but on only those issues of direct concern to the most powerful.[15]

The Scenarios Working Group of the Millennium Assessment agreed that "Order from Strength" is ultimately unsustainable in terms of ecosystems and the societies they support.[16] In the effort to provide for internal security, the measures taken undermine the possibility of poorer countries sustaining their own development, thus increasing resentment and pressure for migration.

B1 Story Line and Scenario Family

The central elements of the B1 future are *a high level of environmental and social consciousness combined with a globally coherent approach to a more sustainable development*. Governments, businesses, the media, and the public pay increased attention to the environmental and social aspects of development. Technological change plays an important role.

Economic development is balanced, and efforts to achieve equitable income distribution are effective. As in A1, the B1 story line describes a fast-changing and convergent world, but the priorities differ. Whereas the A1 world invests its gains from increased productivity and know-how primarily in further economic growth, the B1 world invests a large part of its gains in improved efficiency of resource use ("dematerialization"), equity, social institutions, and environmental protection. Concepts of "green" GDP, gross domestic product, including socially desirable activities such as childcare, apply in particular to the B1 scenario.[17]

A strong welfare net prevents social exclusion on the basis of poverty. However, countercurrents may develop, and in some places people may not conform to the main social and environmental intention. Massive income redistribution and high taxation levels may adversely affect the economic efficiency and functioning of world markets.

Particular effort is devoted to increases in resource efficiency to achieve the goals stated above (efficiency of resource use, equity, social institutions, and environmental protection). Incentive systems, combined with advances in international institutions, permit the rapid diffusion of cleaner technology.[18] Research and Development is also enhanced, together with education and the capacity building for clean and equitable development. Organizational measures are adopted to reduce material wastage by maximizing reuse and recycling. The combination of technical and organizational change yields high levels of material and energy saving, as well as reductions in pollution. Labor productivity also improves as a by-product of these efforts. Alternative scenarios considered within the B1 family include different rates of GDP growth and dematerialization (for example, decline in energy and material intensities).

The demographic transition to low mortality and fertility occurs at the same rate as in A1, but for different reasons, as it is motivated partly by social and environmental concerns. Global population reaches nine billion by 2050 and declines to about seven billion by 2100. High economic activity results in US$350 trillion by 2100, and this world moves deliberately toward international and national income equality. Global income per capita in 2050 averages US$13,000, one-third lower than in A1. A higher proportion of this income is spent on services rather than on material goods, and on quality rather than quantity, because the emphasis on material goods is less and also resource prices are increased by environmental taxation. In contrast to the world of scenario A1, the reduction of income inequalities is not a by-product but rather the result of constant domestic and international efforts.[19]

The B1 story line sees a relatively smooth transition to alternative energy systems as conventional oil and gas resources decline. There is extensive use of conventional and unconventional gas as the cleanest fossil resource during the transition, but the major push is toward post-fossil technologies, driven in large part by environmental concerns.

Environmental quality is high, as most potentially negative environmental aspects of rapid development are anticipated and effectively dealt with locally, nationally, and internationally. For example, transboundary air pollution (acid rain) is basically eliminated in the long term. Land use is managed carefully to counteract the impacts of activities potentially damaging to the environment. Cities are compact and designed for public and nonmotorized transport, with suburban developments tightly controlled. Strong incentives for low-input, low-impact agriculture, along with maintenance of large areas of wilderness, contribute to high food prices with much lower levels of meat consumption than those in A1. These proactive local and regional environmental measures and policies also lead to relatively low GHG emissions, even in the absence of explicit interventions to mitigate climate change.

The Millennium Assessment version of B1 is "Techno-Garden." Recognizing the importance of ecosystem services, a range of ecological property rights are formalized, assigned to communal groups, states, individuals, and corporations. These rights provide some incentive for ecosystem engineering to protect and maintain the ecosystem service and to ease industrial countries away from protective subsidies. Developing countries then have opportunities for agricultural trade: Eastern Europe, Africa, and Latin America enjoy opportunities to produce for the global agricultural market and enjoy increased income.

Europe and North America respond to concern for ecology and shift agricultural production away from high volume of single crops to another model, multiple crops characterized by multifunctionality, profitable though lower-yield production of food and fiber and a range of ecosystem services appropriate for each landscape. Diversification of agricultural production and lower yields encourage the profitability of smaller-scale farming. Genetically modified crops prove to be relatively safe, so the European Union drops its resistance to them.

Developing nations' intensive agricultural practices are not as sensitive to ecological concerns, so some degradation occurs; water pollution and eutrophication (nutrient pollution) of fresh and coastal waters, deforestation, and erosion become significant problems.

Local, rural, and indigenous cultures are overridden by the highly managed "urban garden" approach reflecting functional values. The degree of biodiversity loss varies from region to region, and the result is a lowering of the adaptive capacity of local ecosystems. However, sensitive and cheap ecological monitoring allows for the rapid accumulation of short-term ecological knowledge. Ecosystem services tend to be simplified, because the more obscure and apparently unimportant processes are not understood and not sustained. Loss of ecosystem complexity leads to the increased risk of a major ecological breakdown. Sometimes the problems created by the new technologies seem to multiply faster than the solutions that can be engineered.

Although in the near term biodiversity loss is decreased, an inadvertent long-term consequence might be that wilderness disappears as "gardening" of nature increases and people have fewer experiences of nature.[20]

B2 Story Line and Scenario Family

The B2 world is one of increased concern for environmental and social sustainability compared to the A2 story line. Increasingly, environmentally aware citizens influence government policies and business strategies at the national and local levels, with a trend toward local self-reliance and stronger communities. International institutions decline in importance, with a shift toward local and regional decision-making structures and institutions. Human welfare, equality, and environmental protection all have a high priority, and they are addressed through community-based social solutions in addition to technical solutions, although implementation rates vary across regions.

On the positive side, this story line appears to be consistent with current institutional frameworks in the world and with the current technology dynamics. On the negative side is the relatively slow rate of development in general, but particularly in the currently developing parts of the world.

Education and welfare programs are pursued widely, which reduces mortality and, to a lesser extent, fertility. The population reaches about ten billion by 2100. Income per capita grows at an intermediate rate to reach about US$12,000 by 2050. By 2100, the global economy might expand to reach some US$250 trillion. International income differences decrease, although not as rapidly as in story lines of higher global convergence.

Local inequity is reduced considerably through the development of stronger community-support networks.

High educational levels promote both development and environmental protection. In fact, environmental protection is one of the few truly international common priorities that remain in B2. Strategies to address global environmental challenges are not of a central priority and are thus less successful compared to local and regional environmental response strategies. The governments have difficulty designing and implementing agreements that combine global environmental protections even when this could be associated with mutual economic benefits.

The B2 story line presents a particularly favorable climate for community initiative and social innovation, especially in view of the high educational levels. Technological frontiers are pushed less than they are in A1 and B1, and innovations are also regionally more heterogeneous. Globally, investment in energy research and development continues its current declining trend, and mechanisms for international diffusion of technology and know-how remain weaker than in scenarios A1 and B1 (but higher than in A2). Some regions with rapid economic development and limited natural resources place particular emphasis on technology development and bilateral cooperation. Technological change is therefore uneven. The high emphasis on environmental protection at the local and regional levels is reflected in faster development and diffusion of energy technologies with lower emissions, including advanced coal technologies, nuclear, and renewables. Solar and wind electricity-generating costs are assumed to decline to U.S. cents 3/KWh.[21]

Land use management becomes better integrated at the local level in the B2 world. Urban and transport infrastructure is a particular focus of community innovation and contributes to a low level of dependence on automobiles and less urban sprawl. An emphasis on food self-reliance contributes to a shift in dietary patterns toward local products, with relatively low meat consumption in countries with high population densities.

Energy systems differ from region to region, depending on the availability of natural resources. The need to use energy and other resources more efficiently spurs the development of less carbon-intensive technology in some regions. Environmental policy cooperation at the regional level leads to success in the management of some transboundary environmental problems, such as acidification caused by sulfur dioxide (SO_2), especially to sustain regional self-reliance in agricultural production. Although globally the energy system remains predominantly hydrocarbon-based to 2100, a gradual transition occurs away from the current share of fossil resources in world energy supply, with a corresponding reduction in carbon intensity.

The MA version of the B2 scenario is called "Adapting Mosaic," because it foresees local, regional, even national experimentation with "actively adaptive management," investigating alternatives through experimentation. In it we see high investment in human and social capital, such as education, training, and the development of cooperative networks. One significant outcome of this emphasis is the strengthening of civil societies and responsiveness of government to citizen pressure. Participatory forms of government increase freedom and choice in poorer countries and in richer nations also.

But little attention is paid to global commons problems, such as climate change, marine fisheries, and transboundary pollution. Ecological feedbacks acting over large areas are too large to be noticed by local institutions, leading to large-scale environmental crises: climate shifts lead to storm surges in coastal areas; coastal pollution leads to degradation of coastal fisheries; top predators vanish from most marine ecosystems leaving jellyfish as the apex predator. Climate change is not as bad as in two other scenarios, because local pollutants such as nitrogen oxides and sulphur dioxide have been curtailed by local and regional measures. The focus on environmental rather than technological solutions leads to lower environmental impacts and slower economic growth.[22]

In this scenario, global business and international governance for trade agreements as well as international environmental management emerge during the mid-twenty-first century, because people learn the need for them. But the international institutions that are rebuilt draw on decades of local and regional successes and failures, and the emerging institutions are more focused on ecosystem units, such as watersheds, air basins, and coastal regions, than on political boundaries, as the basis for management. Even large-scale management focuses on "learning while managing," taking into account successes at local levels.

At midcentury, global ecology will be better than at the beginning of the century, but global environmental problems will be pressing.[23]

Sorting through the Scenarios

The scenario writers have served us well by anticipating these possible futures, using a fairly consistent panel of variables. At this point, I wish to assert authorial guidance to simplify the options with which we should concern ourselves. I recommend we further narrow the options by insisting that our future together be shaped by patterns and practices that protect the following:

- ecological effectiveness, or the capacity to curtail greenhouse gas emissions that lead to climate change;
- sustainable communities, defined as communities rich in social capital and civil society, and adaptive to the ecology in which they are embedded;
- biodiversity, defined as the community of living organisms interacting with one another and with the physical environment, and also referring to the variety of ecosystems in the world.[24]

By themselves, without policies specifically targeted to GHG emissions, no one scenario is sufficient. Here are the anticipated CO_2 concentrations in the atmosphere plus the temperature change in 2100 for each scenario.[25]

Scenario	CO_2 Concentration in Parts per Million and Range	Temperature Change °C
B1	540 ppm (range 486–681)	1.8 °C
A1T	575 ppm (range 506–735)	2.4
B2	611 ppm (range 544–769)	2.4
A1B	703 ppm (range 617–918)	2.4
A2	836 ppm (range 735–1,080)	3.4
A1FI	958 ppm (range 824–1,248)	4.0

These projections are unnerving. In the earlier materials produced by the IPCC, 450 ppm was a kind of standard to approach with an understanding that to keep CO_2 concentrations below this mark the planet could avoid major climate system shifting. But even at the current level (between 390 and 400 ppm in 2009), prolonged drought in Africa, melting polar ice caps, the heat wave in Europe, Hurricane Katrina, prolonged flooding throughout large areas of the U.S. Midwest, severe flooding in Indonesia and Bangladesh, and the number and intensity of California wildfires all indicate that the climate system is experiencing major disruption already, even at levels below 450. Yet the lowest anticipated concentrations of CO_2 in 2100, according to these scenarios, is 540 ppm. It appears that the world needs to kick up several notches the intentionality by which we organize ourselves to deal with our greenhouse gas emissions, and explicit policies to lower emissions will be necessary. The larger question of which path to development should be given our support nevertheless remains, because the policies we design will either encourage or frustrate the future, or telos, which will pull us forward.

The A1 story line respresents a world with a high degree of economic globalization, high resource consumption as the dominant definition of wealth, and "nature" managed as a garden primarily for human consumption. Wild nature is not valued or protected for itself, but only as it services human ends. A2, as a regionally focused version of these priorities, is neither ecologically effective nor engendering of sustainable community, so it has little to recommend it. Because in both of these scenarios, biodiversity is a derivative value, secondary to human well-being and instrumental only, I set aside these scenarios to focus on the remaining two.

The B1 and B2 story lines both represent high levels of commitment to protecting the integrity of the various ecologies worldwide. Their approaches are quite different. The B1 vision of the world depends more on globally coordinated economic and environmental policies and enjoys high levels of per capita income. One might make the case for B1 on the basis that the high levels of income per capita will have a more positive effect on the eradication of human poverty and hunger.[26] Furthermore, the human population level of seven billion by 2100 is a big advantage, compared to ten billion in the B2 scenario. Finally, B1 enjoys the lowest level of greenhouse gas emissions of all the scenarios.

The flexibility mechanisms of the Kyoto Protocol, by which the large energy corporations are provided with incentives to get on board in decreasing CO_2, are consistent with the B1 vision. This scenario family takes seriously that global problems require global solutions, and that the economic and political power of large nonstate actors cannot be curtailed by nation-states acting alone. On the grounds of ecological effectiveness, therefore, B1 shines.

Yet B1 fails on the criterion of sustainable community, and in the long term it fails on biodiversity also. It puts its faith and confidence in technological solutions. We have enough history with genetically modified organisms, a practice mentioned within this scenario as an example of the bioengineered adaptation typical of this scenario, to know that their development is tied to the development and marketing of herbicides and high water and nitrogen application. GMOs are developed to benefit corporate vertical control of agricultural processes.[27] The effects of such developments on biodiversity are still of deep concern.

The writers do emphasize the importance in B1 given to movement toward income equality worldwide, which has a basic appeal. It is achieved in large measure through economic and cultural globalization. The globalization envisioned in B1, involving mobile capital and mobile labor, people following the capital to find jobs, has upsides in cross-cultural contact. But the downsides are too great: unaccountability of capital to the requirements of sustainable communities, in terms of effluents left behind, unemployment, and the weakening of a sense of belonging to a community, where social capital is grown.

The B2 story line reflects aware citizenship applying pressure on government and business policies at local, regional, and national levels, and while economic growth rates are lower than in the other story lines, the shift away from international institutions and toward local and regional decision making is distinctive to this scenario. The responses to environmental challenges are crafted at the local and regional levels, and wild nature is protected rather than gardened, primarily through the limitation on land development and urban and suburban sprawl. The economy is more localized than in the B1 scenario, as illustrated by the dependence on local agriculture and low meat consumption.

But the strength of the B2 scenario is the scale of economic, political, and social organization; because it is more rooted in geographies, it provides the capacity for local self-reliance, stronger communities, and local and regional decision making. This scale is a prerequisite for the growing up of citizens, as "citizens" have more capacities for problem solving in local contexts than do "consumers."

The population differential between B1 (seven billion in 2100) and B2 (ten billion in 2100) is significant. Yet the impact on the global life support systems via technology and affluence will not be as high as in the B1 lifestyle. The B2 scenario is not devoid of technological diffusion of efficient energy production, and the scale of energy and environmental protection remains local and regional. The power to affect the shape of the community's response to food, energy, transportation, and housing needs is grown on the local and regional level.

Economically, the B2 scenario envisions strong local economies, enabling communities to be sustainable in the sense that they have more resources than would be available to them in the international corporate-based economy. With those resources communities are better prepared to address specific problems such as the provision of health care, adequate housing, clean water and sanitation, and response to disasters. Large and small communities need strong economies to adapt to changing conditions, whether natural or otherwise.[28]

I argue the B2 vision of the future should provide the basic outlines of the social telos, or goal, for political and ecological striving. However, it needs the international and national mechanisms such as are already operable in the Kyoto Protocol as a way of incentivizing large energy, cement, and automobile players, whose impacts cannot be effectively regulated at the local and regional levels alone. But what is visionary in the B2 scenario, and the reason we should let it frame our peek into the future, is the picture of communities engaged in shaping their local responses to their ecologies and to climate phenomena in a site-specific manner. In effect, though initially B1 is more effective in lowering GHGs, B2 is more effective in sustaining communities and biodiversity. But it will take engaged citizens to make the necessary transitions to new definitions of "the good life."

The case for B2 with its local and regional focus is not a slam dunk. B1 has much to recommend it.

What happens if we add a fourth criterion into the panel of norms to bring to the assessment of possible futures? In addition to ecological effectiveness, sustainable communities, and biodiversity, what if we add "coherence with the New Testament witness?" What would close attention to the Gospels and Paul's letters do to inform our contemporary moral deliberation on what is a good life? These questions are specific to communities rooted in Christian tradition. It is to these questions we now turn, recognizing that the project of using ancient texts to inform contemporary moral deliberation requires some sensitivities to methodological concerns, which is the topic of the next chapter.

PART TWO

Reading the Bible
and Doing Ethics

CHAPTER FOUR

The Bible and Ecological Ethics

Which vision of the world should guide the climate change policies we choose may on the surface appear to be matters of subjective preference. But because these choices have consequences that are global in scope, are rooted in values and visions that conflict in significant degrees with others' values and visions, and signify very different levels of access to the means of securing livelihood for humans and for other creatures, they are moral matters. In the sense that the choices are matters of moral choice, they trump preferences. They might also be considered religious matters, because the choices depict different versions of what is ultimately real and worthy of valuing.

Granting the normative claim that moral responsibility requires industrialized nations to take action to lower GHGs significantly, and granting that the measures to implement this goal must seem just/fair, if for no other reason than to gain cooperation on a wide scale, the question turns to "How?" The Special Report on Emissions Scenarios shows us four different paths to the future. The futures are so different, particularly considering the levels of global population, per capita income, and whether biodiversity is protected; surely the commitment to one future rather than the others is "toned" by religious sensitivities.

If so, then it is a good thing to pause on the question of how religious perspectives function to tone our moral muscles. In this case, I ask how the New Testament texts can affect Christians' moral sensitivities. This investigation will be more normative than empirical. That is, it is a worthwhile project to investigate how Christian tradition *has* affected Christians' attitudes and practices, and not enough empirical work has been done on this question. I hope more will be done in the near future. But in this project, the approach is to ask how reading the New Testament texts in a certain way, sensitive to social structural dynamics that prompted the writing of the texts and are promoted in the texts, might have an impact on the values Christians would advocate should be given priority in choosing our futures. This approach is consistent with the IPCC's Scenario tree. Just as it is futile to consider "the environment" in the absence of attention to population, the economy, energy, technology, agriculture, and our contribution, religion, so also it is futile to read the Bible as a resource in ecological ethics without attention to those driving forces affecting the people of the ancient texts.

The Scope of the Project of Social Ethics

There are so many ways in which people engage the process of moral reflection, many of them marked by deep integrity. Often coming to clarity involves steps that are difficult to identify or cannot be precisely described. Moreover, the moral life is much broader than making decisions in moments of conflict. It can involve general predispositions to facing life with certain attitudes that must be cultivated. Or the moral life might better be described as developing certain sensibilities, capacities for feeling with others, rather than decision making in the face of "problems."

Yet there are times when we should name and confront "problems" and work cooperatively with others to figure out "the right thing to do." If we have good reason to believe that the patterns of economic and political relationships are not life promoting, social ethical reflection is needed to prompt the consideration of alternative values, policies, and common practices. Social ethics involves reflecting on institutions and other structures, systems, and patterns of power in order to develop clarity about who receives benefits from such patterned relationships and who pays their costs or suffers their harms. Social ethics almost always leads to intrapsychic conflict as well as to social dispute. Since no society on earth is egalitarian, every social system rewards differentially and exacts suffering differentially, some more than others. No social order can function without people internalizing the purported rightness of that order, which is why proposals for change almost always produce anxiety. Since the focus of this work is a situation in which the benefits and harms of atmospheric pollution are not distributed equally, simply describing the situation is bound to elicit conflictual feelings, reflecting some kind of recognition that patterns of relationship around the globe should change. But how should they change? In classrooms, church study groups, county boards of supervisors, state legislatures, and national parliaments, there is today genuine disagreement about how the public should organize itself to distribute the goods and harms of atmospheric pollution. Since this question has a bearing on the life or death of the biosphere, we should pay attention.

"Paying attention" to "decisions" is a multifaceted process involving determining how issues are defined, what values should have priority, what data are used, how those data are analyzed, on whose behalf (with what loyalties) decisions are to be made, how "right making" is understood (as determined by consequences, context, inherent rights and wrongs or duties and obligations, character and virtues), the authorities to which people appeal, whether space is left for free action, and what motives drive actors' behavior.

All these factors are involved in ethical reflection. Given all that goes into the process of ethical deliberation, and given all the points at which disagreement can reside and prevent consensus, social ethics is necessarily a wide endeavor. This chapter delves most deeply into only one of these factors, the issue of authority when the Bible plays a role in the shaping of attitudes and patterns of behavior in social, political, and economic relationships. It has often been said that the Bible never plays as important a role in moral reflection as Christians claim, but instead is used to justify positions taken on other grounds. That may be. But because the Bible is meaning-bearing for so many people, and has been authoritative in positive as well as harmful ways, it is an arena of struggle to do biblical interpretation as a part of moral deliberation. Though I will focus on the Bible as a resource, or authority, in ecological ethics, I do so only assuming that all the other factors involved in moral reflection described above must nevertheless receive their due.

Using Scripture in Ethics

What does it mean to explore the New Testament for perspectives that might help with moral bearings in regard to implementing climate change policy? I hardly need to say that global warming is not a topic addressed in the New Testament. Yet that does not now, nor has it ever, stopped Christians facing questions of survival from looking to these texts as a resource for what our job description is.[1]

As a twenty-first-century person who wants to understand Jesus of Nazareth and his movement, and what the apostle Paul contributed to the Jesus movement, approaching the Bible as the main source of perspectives and stories about him and them, I face more than a few difficulties. Most obvious are the problems of getting reliable sources about the persons, the movements attached to them, and the times. Two historians from the first century, Josephus and Philo, mention Jesus and events that affected him, but these sources are scant. The oldest materials in the New Testament are the letters of Paul, from the middle of the first century, and Paul did not know Jesus of Nazareth, who was killed around 30 C.E. Paul's encounter with the risen Christ occurred around 32 C.E.[2] The stories about Jesus recounted in the Synoptic Gospels and John came from the Jesus movement but were compiled and edited with significant variations around 70–90 C.E., after the destruction of the Second Temple. The gospelers knew that the Romans had quelled the Jewish resistance in 60–67, and they had little incentive to associate the Christian communities with the destroyed temple.

Finally, each of the gospelers had a theology and an agenda that affected the organization and editing of the stories. Each Gospel has its own narrative logic and representation of the person Jesus, and each has its own audience, a community with political and social dynamics. It is a disservice to attempt to harmonize the Gospel texts with one another—and certainly with the Pauline letters—because pluralism of voices is intrinsic to the New Testament, just as it is to the Hebrew Scriptures. The audience of the Gospel texts changed from the context in which Jesus spoke to Palestinian villagers face-to-face. The audience for the written texts were urban people who spoke Greek.[3] Surely knowing something about the original audiences will complicate the way we hear the words of the written texts. These are routine difficulties for any Christian reader of the texts, and in this regard Christian ethicists are not unique. Yet by virtue of being a Christian ethicist, and not solely a philosophical ethicist, I must be accountable in some way to the authority of the Scriptures. The exact manner of accountability is always an open question. About this Christians have a tradition inherited from our Israelite relatives of reflecting together, and frequently arguing with each other, with the texts, and with God.

Avoiding Anachronism and Ethnocentrism

The difficulty of avoiding anachronism and ethnocentrism can *never* be overestimated.[4] We need to guard against imposing twenty-first-century industrialized and individualist cultural assumptions back into first-century Palestine when there is good anthropological and historical evidence that such assumptions were not embedded in those earlier meaning systems (and to import them would be anachronistic). And we must be alert to the danger of assuming that my culture is universal, such that what makes my place and people-of-location understandable is the key to understanding all others (ethnocentrism). Guarding against anachronism and ethnocentrism requires a large community of accountability, however, a community constituted by people with enough other-culture perspective to help identify the assumptions that in effect are the air we breath. That other-culture perspective might be rooted in social-scientific disciplines and/or in lived-world experience of another time, gender, class, "race," and place. While I believe we must hold fast the goal of reading the biblical texts free from anachronism and ethnocentrism, and to one degree or another failure is inevitable, I nevertheless accept the discipline of being open to criticism when I fail and seek help to keep that failure in the smaller degrees. Bill Countryman's words are of some comfort: "Perfection will never be possible in this effort, but it is not necessary either."[5]

The effort to avoid anachronism and ethnocentrism when reading biblical texts is what Fernando Segovia calls "distantiation," emphasizing the cultural and historical remoteness of the text.[6] Distantiation is an important and necessary process that allows biblical texts to be recognized as having their own points of view, strategic concerns, and contexts in historical and cultural matrices, all of which may be very different from those of contemporary readers. Reading the Bible thus involves intercultural criticism, acknowledging the otherness of the authors of the texts and the people of the world behind the texts. It represents a form of intercultural awareness, a necessary step before intercultural dialogue can develop. Without the distantiation that makes intercultural awareness possible, the reader will get out of the biblical texts exactly what she or he brings to them.

Bruce Malina has attempted to understand the world of first-century Palestine through cultural anthropology, and identifies three self-evident truths characteristic of that time, but which challenge the self-evident truths of industrialized societies. These truths were assumed by the writers of the first-century texts, Paul, Mark, Luke, Matthew, and John: the conviction of the futility of extra effort or labor; the common experience that no one suffers inordinately or dies for lack of the necessities of life ("Consider the lilies of the field, how they grow; they neither toil nor spin" [Matt 6:28][7]); the fact of the wickedness of the wealthy.[8] If Max Weber was right, in cultures imbued or infused with Calvinism, such as are many segments of the United States, Canada, Australia, and some European countries, the Protestant ethic contradicts all three of these truths that were self-evident to Jesus and his neighbors.[9] If we are unaware of the different worldviews involved, we will inevitably read them anachronistically and ethnocentrically.

In this vein, we in the twenty-first century are adapted to social/analytical practices that identify religious factors, political factors, kinship factors, and economic factors operative in a particular social context. This way of looking at the social body may not be shared by our first-century forebears. For them, kinship and politics were the only two institutionalized patterns of relating. What we might view as "religion" and "economics" were embedded in kinship systems and political systems.

What are the consequences of these different assumptions? What the twenty-first century means by separation of church and state would be a legacy of the eighteenth century, completely foreign to the first century. Further, it would be anachronistic to look to the Scriptures for their "purely spiritual" meaning. The ancient Mediterranean world had no separate institutionalized practices for religion.[10] Rather, religion was an overarching meaning system that unified political, kinship, and embedded economic systems into an ideological whole. It would legitimate or challenge political power structures and family dynamics.

Similarly, first-century Palestine had no distinctive institutional practices for what might be called macro-economics. The family was a producing unit as well as a consuming unit. Economics was more embedded in the household than is typical of households in industrialized societies, which are primarily consumption oriented (setting aside the production function of childbearing for the moment). Kings and lords were persons who had complete power over persons and things in their domain, and they were entitled to use any products or properties of the realm.[11] Economics was in this sense subsumed into political rulership and kinship relations.

What is the consequence of economics being embedded in kinship and political systems? If we are to ask the Scriptures what bearing they might have on contemporary climate change policies, particularly those that use economic measures, we will have to be sensitive to practices "embedded" in kinship and/or politics.

Many methods of reading the Bible are useful to help us regard the texts as socially, culturally, and historically other than ourselves. These methods include historical criticism, use of social sciences (for instance, to identify the indigenous caste system), and literary and cultural criticism. Because each of these methods selects aspects of the texts to foreground and runs risks of incompleteness, humility is always a virtue in biblical interpretation, as is collegiality.

Drawing Analogies

But after distantiation, no text can be a resource for the contemporary world unless some similarities can be found. For without some common points of reference, the Scriptures are not normative in any way. The process of sifting relevance of Scriptures for the later reader requires drawing accurate analogies from the texts to the twenty-first century, or from this time to that one. The key word here is "accurate," and accuracy represents a big difficulty—because not only do we need some categories by which to understand the ancient world, but we also need to understand the current context and the dynamics that brought us to this point in terms of these same categories.

Marvin Chaney has used to good advantage the herme-neutical process of "dynamic analogy," a term that acknowl-edges that no analogy is ever totally accurate. Every analogy highlights certain similarities but eventually breaks down. The method of drawing dynamic analogy avoids two problems: universalizing messages in biblical texts by ignoring the plu-ralism of political and theological agendas represented by the different texts; and antiquarian particularism, which traps the reader in the specifics of each historical situation, unable to see patterns that might be shared across the eras. Between these extremes lies a "generic middle," categories of meaning that are part of the immediate cultural experience of broad classes of people and are characteristic of different places, events, times, and cultures.[12] Comparative cultural anthropology and other social sciences help readers identify generic similarities, if they exist, among different cultures, and this perspective has already been tapped earlier in this chapter and will be used more in chapters 5 through 7.

Chaney recommends to his students that they read the Deuteronomistic History (Deuteronomy–2 Kings) with their Assyrian hats on. In terms of power dynamics, the United States is the modern counterpart not of Judah but of Assyria. It is the United States that has viewed and used other, smaller nations as pawns and surrogates, just as Assyria did.[13] The Deuteronomis-tic History offers trenchant commentary on the history of U.S. relations with smaller countries; but then the Elohistic texts challenge the Deuteronomistic texts, and the dynamic anal-ogy shifts to another aspect of similarity between ancient Israel and the contemporary United States. Similarly the Priestly and Yahwistic perspectives will bring a different perspective. Hearing the differences in the pluralistic collection is a neces-sary step in making analogies, as is acknowledgment that all approaches are partial and conditioned by the contexts they address. None alone is adequate or sufficient for all contexts.

The various perspectives complement, supplement, and correct one another only as we allow them to be different. Chaney concludes that pluralism may be a theological problem, but it is also a theological resource, and one that might help us move beyond factionalism.[14]

Because drawing analogies may seem a very thin thread to connect the ancient texts to the contemporary world, let us consider some of the alternatives. Richard Hays suggests that, in addition to the descriptive task already described above—the historical-critical approach—readers should use key themes that arise inductively from reading the texts, and through a synthetic process discern a "truth" that can be shared by ancient people and the contemporary world. Hays suggests three "focal images" that offer coherence among the loose collection of documents that make up the New Testament: community, cross, and new creation. Whatever themes or focal images are suggested, Hays says, they should be widely represented in *all* the canonical texts, not stand in serious tension with any of the New Testament witnesses, and should each highlight central and substantive ethical concerns of the texts in which they appear.[15] These requirements control the choice of focal images by theological criteria rather than by the social dynamics, consistent with dynamic analogy. Moreover, they undermine the possibility of treating the texts as embodying pluralism of voices, even though Hays warns against premature harmonization of the texts.

For instance, the requirement that the focal images be widely represented in *all* the canonical texts rules out using "the reign of God" as an interpretive key, because while this theme is central for Jesus of Nazareth in the Synoptic Gospels and John, it is hardly present in Paul, and it disappears in the later pastoral letters. I therefore conclude that Hays's requirement ends up privileging the Pauline and pseudo-Pauline texts, erasing the conflicting points of view about serious matters that the different texts reflect and hiding from the reader instances in which later writers seem to have introduced material into older texts to change their impact. Nevertheless, Hays acknowledges that an effort at synthesis is definitely required for readers of the Scriptures, and the choice of the controlling themes or images should be a point of discussion and may perhaps be a point of contention.

An additional approach, while acknowledging the need for the historical-critical step and some process of synthesis through the use of major controlling themes, also recommends bringing forward the traditions of the churches. Particularly for the confessional churches, attention to the tradition or heritage of the churches through their creeds and confessions is important. Jack Rogers, for example, representing the efforts of the Presbyterian churches to interpret the Bible in matters bearing on contemporary church and society, includes a further guideline for interpretation: "Be guided by the doctrinal consensus of the church, which is the rule of faith." It requires distinguishing between the culturally conditioned practices of the church and the essential teaching of the church found in its creedal statements, which are the "rule of faith."[16] The same process of interpretation by inductive analysis that is involved in reading the Scriptures is therefore required for bringing forward relevant teachings from the tradition.

Serious historical-critical study of the biblical texts, identification of key themes, avoiding false harmonization, attention to the teachings of the tradition—the guidelines for interpretation that Rogers describes as being generated by the Presbyterian churches in the United States—still require analogical thinking. The themes of redemptive activity of God in which Jesus plays a central role in the story; the rule of love: love of God and the neighbor; and creation, fall, and redemption in Jesus Christ, are different from the ones Hays suggests; but consistent with Hays, if particular interpretations are inconsistent with these themes or focal images, the particular interpretations should be overridden.

The heritages of our churches will have an impact on the way controlling themes are determined. Sometimes a major critical overhaul of such "themes" has to happen to help the churches see their situation more accurately and to read their biblical texts and their creeds and confessions in a new light. But the very process of identifying the key messages of the formative texts is a political one, and a good one, if it helps instill the disciplines of historical-critical study broadly among the faithful.

Our Questions May Skew Our Reading

A further difficulty that dogs my efforts to understand the Bible as a resource for moral reflection is that I have a question about which I hope to find some direction or perspectives. My government, our governments, direct our negotiators to participate cooperatively, or not, to stabilize and then lower harmful industrial-era effects on the air envelope and climate. While I, like my students and others in democratic nations, have formal rights to pressure our elected representatives to take stands, the policy-making process on climate change has not been transparent. Christian denominational and para-denominational bodies will either press policy-makers to be more responsive to the urgency of the problem of climate change that confronts our earth, or we will collude with corporate and governmental agencies that resist the limitations on their freedom that such climate change policy will represent. It is interesting to me that when Christians come together in an ecumenical and international forum, to which we bring concerns specific to our places, we also come with some shared traditions, one of which is to read the Bible. As different and unique are our approaches to worship, theologizing, and scriptural interpretation, we still share a practice involving reading from the texts together, looking for what we might call the word of God to us for this time. The biblical texts are a shared resource. Yet, by virtue of the fact that we are bringing specific questions to the text, we run the risk of approaching Jesus of Nazareth as a "reflecting surface" to understand our twenty-first-century challenge. Herein lies the grand difficulty of the entirety of this essay. But it is a difficulty that is a gift, because it is one of the ways to acknowledge the power of the readers' experience in shaping the attitudes, dispositions, expectations, and concerns—not to mention panic—that inform our dialogue with the Scriptures.

The Approach of This Project

Aware of the cultural and historical conditioning of biblical texts, alert to the pitfalls of making erroneous analogies from the texts, acknowledging the provisional choice of major categories or themes we use to make connections, humbled by the extent to which our questions might skew our reading, readers must also attempt some sensitivity to the ways we ourselves are socially, historically, and, I would say, ecologically conditioned.[17] It is a matter of responsibility to you the reader for me to own (1) my ecological and political location as one who reads the texts, (2) my strategy for reading the Bible, and (3) the theoretical and theological foundations behind this strategy.

Several factors affect the perspective I bring to reading the Bible. I teach Christian social ethics in a Presbyterian-related seminary that belongs to a consortium of nine Protestant and Roman Catholic seminaries on the West Coast of the United States. Ecologically, my teaching takes place in an area of the States that is marked by a Mediterranean climate, one that has a rainy season for five or so months and dry weather the rest of the year. In this regard my context shares something very basic with the first-century Palestinian world, a certain type of climate. On the campus where I teach, I am the faculty member who helped develop a community garden, which began as a class project of the environmental ethics class I teach, and a modest amount of land on campus has been dedicated for this use. Every year when I invite people to declare who is interested in being gardeners, I am asked to describe what a community garden entails. Most people know what a "victory garden" is, where people are granted certain spots to grow their own produce or flowers. Victory gardens are quite appropriate in some contexts. But on campus the model has been to work with others to weed, plant, water, and harvest. This model is a stretch for many, and responses range from curious to delighted, but more often suspicious. I persist in gardening as a campus project, seeing it as a political act to grow healthful food for our own consumption. This urban gardening (well, okay—suburban gardening) challenges the accretions of federal policies favoring fossil fuel dependent agribusiness and global food distribution systems. It is with pleasure that we learn bit by bit how to step aside from those fuel-intensive food systems. We can create an alternative culture of "attending" to the natural processes that give us food. The downside, something else we share with Palestinian farmers, is that we see immediately the consequences of extreme weather events and experience food insecurity. Unlike the first-century farmers, however, if our crops wash out and we have money, we can go to the local farmers' market or grocery store to buy produce.

At the same time, this geographical region, which supports the growing of food nearly year around, is also congested from private automobile use, the result of a concerted effort by oil, highway, and auto interests to dismantle public transportation, plus the sprawl that automobile use makes possible. Car culture undoes whatever positive effects urban and suburban gardeners contribute to their region. It is more difficult to step aside from the policies that promote gas guzzling, but I live in a state that has petitioned the Environmental Protection Agency (EPA) for a waiver so that cars sold in this state would have to meet more stringent emission standards than the federal standards. In spite of the support of the total EPA staff to grant the waiver, the EPA director during the George W. Bush administration declined to grant it, saying that the state of California failed to show the compelling and extraordinary conditions required under the Clean Air Act to grant a waiver.[18] Global warming is an international problem, agency chief Stephen Johnson said. It requires global, not regional, solutions.[19] I have two responses to this rationale. First, he was a member of the administration that refused to accept binding targets for reducing climate changing emissions such as the international Kyoto Treaty requires. Second, in its petition for the waiver, the state made the case that California does face enhanced risks from global warming as water shortages, rising sea levels, increased wildfires all affect California more than other states. In addition, global warming currently causes greater respiratory and cardiovascular disease in California per person than in other states through its impact on air pollution. The impact is due to CO_2 increasing ozone and particulate matter—the unhealthful pollutants in smog—by increasing temperatures and water vapor in the atmosphere, and it increases the most where it is already high. California has six of the ten most polluted cities in the United States and already suffers more air pollution mortality per capita from CO_2 than other states.[20]

California was joined by fifteen other states in seeking the emission waiver to have tougher tailpipe emission regulations, representing more than half of all the automobiles in the nation. Collectively, these states could generate enough economic muscle to influence higher national standards. With the next administration, California and the other interested states were granted the authority to require the higher standards.[21] But the power of the automobile and oil industries in the George W. Bush administration to thwart these states' efforts to decrease automobile emissions is a lesson in the tenacity of the Kingdom of Oil.

Finally, my context is that of a twenty-first-century North American who hoped my nation would ratify the Kyoto Treaty and was disappointed when President George W. Bush withdrew the United States in March 2001. Then came September 11, 2001, a day rooted in part in the politics of oil consumption. If the North American region had taken seriously the challenge of Kyoto, the geopolitical alignments with Middle Eastern nations might have been on the road to flexibility. To date, world leaders have decided to delay the difficult task of reaching a climate change agreement until after the next Conference of the Parties in Copenhagen. Because the U.S. Congress has not enacted authorizing climate legislation, other nations will not make their own pledges. This history of resistance on the federal level to accepting responsibility for the United States' effects on the atmospheric global commons has definitely cast a pall on this nation's moral authority.

In the post-September 11 geopolitical context, it is not silly to fear an apocalypse. Unfortunately, some Christians use New Testament apocalyptic to warrant war, trashing all earth's life support systems, in order to hurry the return of Christ. Christians who are less deranged may nevertheless believe that this life and this earth are of only relative importance, since, they believe, the kingdom of God is to be experienced only after death. This attitude is reflected in the unfortunate but consistent finding of social scientists that the churchgoing public, at least in the United States, is less ecologically concerned than the public at large and that the more evangelical or fundamentalist the Christian, the less ecologically concerned she/he is. For these reasons, the churches and all students of the Bible need to see more work connecting New Testament sources with ecological responsibility.

My teacher Walter G. Muelder said, "The New Testament's relation to present-day moral valuation and decision is penetrating, pervasive, and transforming, and yet it is indirect in the sense that no moral judgments in concrete cases ought to be direct deductions from biblical statements."[22] The process of distantiation and drawing accurate analogies will likely discourage any tendency to direct deduction from biblical statements. The other dimension of his statement is as important, to one degree or another, for people who identify themselves as Christians: the New Testament's influence is penetrating, pervasive, and transforming.

Muelder went on to make the case that because the field of Christian social ethics is interdisciplinary, moral claims must be coherent scientifically, philosophically, and theologically, with no one discipline dictating the coherence. Ecological ethics, like many other ethical foci, relies heavily on biological, climate, and social sciences, uses the tools of philosophical ethics, and then for Christians requires additional attention to Scriptures of the churches. Since doing theology seems to be one of the ways Christians probe and debate the relevance of the Scriptures for contemporary issues, the treatment of Jesus and Paul below will participate in theological discourse.

For purposes of reflecting on climate change policies, I look particularly to the New Testament because I believe that the case has already been made with much success that the Hebrew Scriptures ground ecological responsibility for contemporary Christians in at least three ways. The Genesis creation stories declare that God is the source of all life and the physical support systems that sustain it, and it is to God that we are accountable for the way humans, in our different groups, use the earth's resources for our sustenance. The exodus drama and the covenants that emerged in response to that liberation history explicitly link social justice with peace and with the integrity of creation. Further, the Psalms, Job, and other wisdom writings depict creation as beautiful to God and valued in its wildness, quite independent of its usefulness to humankind.

The New Testament, however, is rarely used as a resource for ecological sensibility, with a few exceptions. One is the cosmic Christ in the hymns of the very early church that used language paralleling the odes to Sophia (Wisdom) to identify Jesus as the Wisdom of God. (See, for instance, Colossians 1:15-20; Ephesians 2:14-16; and John 1:1-18.)[23] Another is the association of Jesus as a prophet of the justice of God, who confirms the prophets' fidelity to the Mosaic covenant as a precondition for social equity and peace, including peace in and with all of nature. We need to be careful not to distinguish too sharply the wisdom materials from the prophetic materials in the Gospels, because—particularly in the Q source, the sayings on which Matthew and Luke drew in addition to Mark—there is no conflict between Jesus the sage and Jesus the prophet. Father God and Mother Wisdom are both fully integrated into Jesus' teachings and ministry.[24]

The approach to the New Testament found here as a basis for reflecting on climate change policy is economic/political/religious, since the issues facing the twenty-first century with respect to use of the atmosphere are being treated internationally primarily with economic tools. These issues involve uneven distributions of power embedded in worldviews that assign meaning and value to "nature" and "other people." (We have to put quotation marks around these words because they are, besides being real, also symbol systems.) Core matters of the New Testament are political-economic in nature, with conflicting politics implied in different "religious" perspectives. The scholarly resources employed are those that highlight the economic/political/religious structures affecting the ministry of Jesus and the mission of the apostle Paul. Other methods to approach the texts may well be valid for other purposes.

The reader may appreciate knowing some theoretical and theological assumptions grounding this work. These "assumptions" have grown out of my research for this book and guided the kind of research I did. In this work Christology affirms that Jesus was a reformer of the temple-state centralized in Jerusalem.[25] He and his small group of followers failed in their task of organizing (for) the reign of God when he was crucified by the Roman Empire, just as many others before him had been crucified when they seriously challenged the Roman patron-client system, which was benefiting the temple-based elites. Jesus' resurrection and the visits he made to his followers revivified their loyalty. But in the period following the crucifixion, Jesus' kingdom task became of secondary significance to the communities gathered in his name. Refocusing their attention on his status, those communities of Judean or Galilean Christians and Greco-Roman Israelites and Christians birthed communities that in time became what we now call, perhaps wrongly, churches. Jesus' task was subordinated to his status as the Messiah/Christ in institutionalized Christianity. Too bad. The kingdom of God still needs to be organized.

I assume a method of giving weight to, or authorizing, Scripture that is modeled by Jesus using Torah. He had a perspective about what is most central to Israelite traditions and cited parts of the text (perhaps an aural text) to trump other parts. Paul did the same thing. We today need to take stances and to argue them on biblical grounds and on other grounds also. Our claims must then pass the test of the commonsense rationality of all who have a stake in the outcome. Climate change is a matter of public policy, and the arenas for addressing it include the churches; but it also includes a wider policy debate, in which Hebrew Scriptures and the New Testament will not be explicitly authoritative. With some exceptions, Jesus addressed people for whom Torah was a shared foundation of the community. In Judea and Galilee, Torah was the foundation of political and economic life. It was the law. That is why the debate over what the law required was a matter of great political and economic import. In local, regional, and international discussions today, however, the law governing emissions is not yet shared because it is even now being shaped.

Christian social ethics is by nature interdisciplinary, and in this instance it will be clear how much my own work depends on the work of people in other disciplines. As one who does not speak or read Greek, Aramaic, or Hebrew, I am dependent on the work of biblical scholars. To link the study of the Bible to contemporary ecological issues, I have read a range of biblical scholarship, deciding which approaches seem coherent with the task of thinking about systems and policies, which is what Christian social ethics entails. I acknowledge my debt to those biblical scholars and draw the implications for the ecological questions I bring to the reading, since those questions are not ones the biblical scholars themselves used to organize their expositions. The biblical scholars I lean on do not agree with each other at every point, and they change their own minds as they go. I *use* their work as a resource in my effort to relate the New Testament texts to the questions of our day because they too are interested in seeing Jesus and the Jesus movement, as well as Paul, as social actors in their own history, which may or may not have analogies to the twenty-first century. The way I have focused their work in this project is to ask of them two questions: How do they see Jesus related to Torah, the prophets, and the temple? If Jesus upholds the Torah and prophets, then we must relate the work we have already done to Hebrew Scriptures. Second, how do they interpret Jesus with respect to the meaning of the kingdom of God? The kingdom is the political and economic standard by which all rule, governance, and order are criticized. I also ask how the apostle Paul contributed to policy analysis, if he did. I ask in this study of Jesus of Nazareth and the apostle Paul whether certain presumptions or predispositions will emerge that have a bearing on how we think about how to distribute the benefits and harms of cleaning the atmosphere.

If it is possible to view more focused images for social organization arising from these texts, this would not necessarily mean that Christians are obligated to reproduce those social norms in current policy. Renita Weems's invitation to readers of the Hebrew Scriptures is worth duplicating for readers of the New Testament: Read the Bible in a way that gives you space to question the biblical writers, to recognize the choices they made in shaping their message, and to weigh the vision the writers offer. Engage the writers of the texts in lively conversations. If the visions they offer are not worth devoting your energy to implementing, critique them and resist them. If, on the other hand, the writers of the texts speak the truth, one that is emerging as coherent with other ways of knowing, then participate with the *ekklēsia* in embodying that truth in ways relevant to our times. Always, readers have the right to reject living in worlds that diminish our humanity[26] and our embeddedness in the web of life.

I hope I have made myself transparent as a reader of the biblical texts and author of this essay, someone with certain purposes, goals, and commitments that function as I approach the Bible. The three chapters that follow are my attempt to dialogue with the New Testament in the effort to broaden the possibilities of using the Bible as a resource in thinking about climate change policy.

CHAPTER FIVE

Jesus, Torah, and Temple

The search for the historical Jesus is producing opportunities for all the theological disciplines to rethink their truisms in light of possible new interpretations of the biblical texts. The New Testament scholars who are searching for the historical Jesus are exemplary in their interdisciplinarity, dependent as they are upon archaeology, architecture, historical studies, sociology, economic anthropology, cultural anthropology, and peasant studies, as well as literary and close textual reading. The number of scholars who have come to the conclusion that Jesus of Nazareth is a prophet (in addition to or instead of being a sage, or instead of being a priestly pretender) is particularly impressive.[1] The signs he performed, healings and exorcisms, were his use of power; and in exercising it he called into question a monopoly held by the temple priests. His healings and exorcisms forced the questions of who channels God's power, who mediates God's mercy and forgiveness, and on whose behalf God's power is exercised.[2]

Jesus was an artisan in the peasant class,[3] a layperson, very probably not among the 2 percent of the population who could read or write, though as a carpenter he may have had the use of business Greek. Most of the people whom he taught and healed were peasants living in villages. Some evidence suggests that, at that time in Palestinian society, the extended family had begun to break down as the primary unit, as landholding became more difficult because of debt. Thus, poorer, smaller families became more common. Jesus seems to have been concerned to support the commensal relationships in village life whereby people's needs were met in reciprocal relations of sharing food and other resources, including honor.

There are good reasons to believe that Jesus was critical of the role of the Jerusalem temple and its priests in the whole fabric of Galilean and Judean life. Many of these reasons are based on inferences from efforts at historical reconstruction, and some depend on our reading of the biblical texts.

Jesus Was from Galilee

Jesus was Galilean. The temple, however, was in Jerusalem, the central city of Judea. The regions of Galilee and Judea were both rooted in Israelite Torah, but, unlike Judea, Galilee did not have a long history of having been centrally administered by the temple-state. Galilee had been forcibly annexed to Hasmonean Judea during the administration of Alexander Jannaeus at the beginning of the first century B.C.E. In Jesus' generation, the priests of the temple and their agents were attempting to secure consistent Galilean support of the temple through holy day pilgrimages, tithes, and sacrifices. But the Galilee had a much shorter and shallower identity with the temple than did Judea and Jerusalem.[4]

Galilee and Judea Had Different Histories

No single phenomenon serves as the "pivot point to channel" a different history for the Galilee from that of Judea. But the different histories went way back and can be described at three points. First, in the eighth century B.C.E. (733–732), the Assyrians deported the rulers, officers and retainers, and artisans and merchants of the northern kingdom (which included the Galilee). They left a productive population of people on the land to serve as a province to Assyria, administered by Assyrian officers to gather taxes. For the next six centuries the Israelites in Galilee had a history that was separate and different from the Judeans. The Babylonians and Persians continued to administer the Galilee separately from Judea. The Hellenistic and Roman empires after them ruled Judea through native aristocracies, including previously existing kingships and priesthoods. But no ruling group existed in Galilee, so imperial officials administered the area. The cities in the Galilee did not have as far a reach into the lives of villagers as did cities in Judea, so villagers of Galilee were free to continue patterning their lives according to indigenous customs.[5]

Second, Judea had had the experience of the successful "Maccabean Revolt," the cross-class resistance against the Seleucid troops who attempted to enforce the hellenizing of the temple. The defeat of the Seleucids and the rededication of the temple in Jerusalem served to deepen the identity of Judeans with the integrity of the temple. The Hasmoneans who led that revolt were then appointed to the high priesthood, melding cultic power with their civil power. The Hasmonean dynasty was remembered as the last period of self-government in the land of Israel (164–63 B.C.E.).[6] But the Galilee did not experience the same pressure to hellenize, nor did Galilee have the experience of victory symbolized by the temple. This factor represents another way in which the Galilee and Judea had different histories.

Third, in the century prior to Jesus' birth, Hasmoneans extended their economic and political power north into Galilee and the Golan. After many centuries of Galilean independence from Jerusalem, the Hasmoneans established outposts in the Galilee, Judeans with connections to the Jerusalem aristocracy serving as administrators of Galilee as a province. Officers of the Hasmoneans amassed large landholdings around those outposts, appropriating ancestral holdings from small farmers. While the Galileans shared with Judeans loyalty to the laws of Moses, the prophetic traditions, the practices of festivals, circumcision, and other aspects of Israelite tradition, they probably did not share the Hasmoneans' enthusiasm for the Jerusalem temple and its priests.

The Second Temple Was Associated with Herod

The Second Temple was enhanced and enlarged during a construction project of Herod the Great, who was a client of the Roman Empire. Rome did not govern its empire primarily by means of occupying troops. It had strike forces concentrated at certain points that could be deployed quickly, however, so the threat of military force was ever-present. The primary means of administering the empire was through client kings. Herod secured the compliance of the Hasmoneans by marrying Mariamme, the granddaughter of the high priest Hyrcanus, in 42 B.C.E., with whom he had children. Herod put many of Judea's resources into expanding the temple because of its importance in legitimating the state and attracting business, pilgrims, and other travelers to Jerusalem. After a period of years, however, Herod desired to use the politics of marriage again to acquire wider territory, and he had the princess Mariamme murdered (29 B.C.E.), and later her children and her younger brother, Aristobulus, whom he had appointed high priest in 35 B.C.E. Thus ended the Hasmonean line. While the Hasmonean loyalists had attempted to adapt to Roman rule using a number of mechanisms, including intermarriage, the basis for alliance with Herod's faction proved illusory. One way Hasmonean loyalists thereafter showed their resistance to Herod was to name their babies with names that signaled Judean nationalism: John, Simon, Judas, Salome, and Mariamme, a version of which is Mary.[7] Since Mark (6:3) indicates Jesus' mother, Mary, named his brothers James, Joses, Judas, and Simon, we may have a clue here that Mary had Hasmonean heritage.

The Legitimacy of the High Priest Was Tainted

Multiple sources, along with New Testament passages, attest that the first century was marked by a vigorous diversity of interpretations of right practice in the temple and in the whole society. Sadducees, Pharisees, Essenes, and the Therapeutae, in addition to Jesus and his followers, contended with each other about the correct understanding of the Law and the Prophets. Such diversity was facilitated by the question of the legitimacy of the high priest and his family. Herod the Great did not belong to the subgroup of the tribe of Levi, which was biblically designated to serve in the temple, but once he seized the Hasmoneans' power, he treated the office of high priest as a political appointment and retained control of the high priestly vestments. After 6 C.E. Augustus ruled that the Roman governor of Judea would exercise Herod's old prerogatives and appoint or remove the temple high priest as well as supervise control of his sacred vestments. When Pontius Pilate was prefect of the region (26–36 C.E.), Joseph Caiaphas was the appointed high priest. Pilate governed through the high-priestly houses that controlled the temple. The popular classes (70 to 80 percent of the population) mistrusted the high priestly families because they were collaborators with the Romans, because they accumulated land, and because they did not come from the legitimate priestly line.[8]

These different histories, the perception that the temple priests were colluding with the Romans for their own benefit, and the debates within Israel about what covenant faithfulness meant all add up to indicate a strong likelihood that the Jesus movement presented some kind of separation from or challenge to the temple. But how these deep fissions affected Galileans' practices vis-à-vis the temple is by no means clear. Christians, whose main information about Jesus is from the New Testament, may for reasons of our own cultures, misread the nature of Jesus' relationship to the temple and downplay his loyalty. One particular question serves as the focus for most

Christian ethicists' depiction of Jesus and the temple: Did he challenge the purity system or not?

Jesus Challenged the Temple as the Site of Purification

The first-century historian Josephus notes that the people of Israel from the Galilee, Judea, and the Diaspora knew their ancestral laws; they kept Sabbath, circumcision, and food laws and loyally supported the temple with the half-shekel (or two drachmas) temple tax. Christian theologians may ignore the evidence that Jesus too kept the purity regulations of the Torah, in part because we mistake the purity code as a remedy for sin. According to the purity code, impurity is not sin. The remedy for impurity is purification, not forgiveness. Further comment is in order.

Worship at the temple in Jerusalem in the first century, like almost all, if not all, ancient religious systems, involved blood sacrifice. This included the slaughter of animals and the ritual redistribution of their bodies: some parts were burned on the altar to God; the priests ate some parts; and other parts were distributed to the worshipers. Since proximity to God's altar meant, in some sense, proximity to holiness as well, "whoever approached the altar would have undergone rites of purification that would have included water rituals, abstention from sex, fasting, or avoidance of certain foods."[9] We know about these purification rituals because they are described in the opening books of the Bible and reflected in the Mishnah and Talmud compiled between 200 and 600 C.E. Therefore Jews anywhere in the world could know the purity rules.[10]

Scripture assumes that everyone would be in a condition of impurity at some point, perhaps even most of the time. But Scripture also prescribes the means to remove impurity. One washed and waited until sunset for seven days, or for forty days, depending on the case.[11] If one prepared a deceased relative for final rites, one had touched death and so was impure but had done nothing wrong. There were impurities from evil intention, which did have moral significance, but most impurities were from sources over which one had little or no control, such as ejaculation, menstruation, childbirth or miscarriage, or various other genital emissions. Diseases and the bodies of some animals could also convey impurity through either contact or in some cases proximity. These impurities were objective but usually temporary and not sinful.

Because some purity laws regulated access to the temple, the period preceding the major celebrations involving pilgrimage to the temple (Passover, Shavuot, and Sukkot) would require attention to purification. If pilgrims arrived in Jerusalem too late, they would not be there for the purification rites, so they could not enter God's temple to bring the sacrifice; nor could they eat it.

Before modern Christians argue too strongly that Jesus' ministry took aim at the purity code, it should be acknowledged there is evidence that he kept the laws. In Mark 1:40-44, Jesus cures a leper by touching him and then orders the man to show himself to the priest and offer the sacrifices as Moses commanded (in Leviticus 14:1-32). In the Sermon on the Mount (Matthew 5:23-24), Jesus instructs his followers how they should offer at the temple. In the Gospels, Jesus goes to Jerusalem for pilgrimage festivals at Passover, at Sukkot, at an unspecified feast, and for a celebration of the Maccabees purifying the temple. He was in Jerusalem for Passover when he was arrested and later executed.

In Mark 7:1-23 Jesus' attitude to the Judaic dietary laws is different from his attitude as presented in Matthew 15:1-20. But Paul's letter to the Galatians describes Peter and Paul arguing about whether Jewish Christians should eat non-kosher food. "If," Paula Fredriksen says, "Jesus had abrogated the food laws during his ministry, apparently neither his own disciples nor Paul himself knew, because neither invoked that teaching to settle the argument."[12] She also argues that purity corresponds neither to social class nor to relationships of gender domination. Leviticus and Numbers provide plenty of evidence of a gender system, but not one of male domination.

How does Fredriksen understand the reason the priests colluded with Rome to have Jesus executed? The priests colluded with Rome, she agrees, but not because Jesus challenged the purity code and the temple's authority in enforcing it.[13] Her main contention is that Jesus and his followers represented a reform movement within temple Judaism; the Jesus movement was one movement among others, all participating in the system about which they disputed.[14]

Distantiation is hard. Clearly, purity systems are "foreign" to twenty-first-century Protestants, such as myself, and it is a stretch to understand the Israelite pollution rites on their own terms. On the other hand, an analogy lurks, waiting to be noticed, for something like a purity system functions today, even in liberal democratic industrialized societies that pretend to be neutral on religious matters in public policy. It takes the form of an emotional response to "difference," codified formally and informally in "race," class, and gender relations. These pollution systems have everything to do with access to social and economic power. It may be dangerous, because anachronistic, to read from contemporary pollution systems back to the Second Temple, but, on the other hand, it is naïve to deny that Galilee and Judea were marked by conflictual relations. This conflict had economic, political, and ecological dimensions, and evidence of this conflict erupts in the Scriptures.

Jesus Recommended to Peasants an Alternative Way to Discharge Their Temple Debts

The temple in Jerusalem facilitated proper circulation of people and animals around the land. It was a slaughterhouse. The temple complex was built to channel Israelites with their produce, including animals, as sacrifices to the priests. The temple was for people to walk *through*.

> In the indigenous idiom of circulation, one is a Jew—
> an Israelite, a Levite, a priest—by virtue of the way one
> moves through this design [of the Temple courtyard

and gates]. Being a Jew means stepping away from Gentiles [going through the Court of Gentiles], through the
mothers [going through the Court of Women], with the
produce of one's land, toward observance of Covenant
obligations, and then receiving back a proper portion of
the produce and carrying it home. The Temple accommodates and defines this motion.[15]

The central importance of the Jerusalem temple in Jesus' day
was established only after the shutting down of other cultic
sites. In the process of shifting obligations to the Jerusalem
temple, for the first time gendered space was instituted for Jewish worship. The Court of the Women, beyond which women
could not proceed, except to the north gate, the Nicanor Gate,
was where women accused of having adultery were required
to appear for the rite of *sotah*, as prescribed in Numbers 5:11-
31; where women were purified after childbirth; and where
recovery of lepers was certified.[16]

We gain additional perspective on the temple by tracing
where bodies would walk—gendered bodies, well and encum-
bered bodies, human and animal bodies—how they circulated
in the arena of the temple, in Jerusalem, and in Judea. This is
the temple into which Herod the Great poured many of the
people's resources as he consolidated his power as client king
to the Romans.

Therefore, a second line of inquiry into the Jesus behind
the Gospels examines the question: Did Jesus challenge the
flow of goods and resources through the temple, or not? The
temple tax netted a large treasury, over which the temple
priests exercised control.[17] Jesus is depicted in Matthew 17:24
as supporting the payment of this tax. "The collectors of the
half-shekel tax went up to Peter and asked, 'Does not your
teacher pay the tax?' He said, 'Yes.'"

It is likely that, the level of taxes and tributes being what
it was, Galilean peasants in large numbers may have let the
temple tax go unpaid. Whether they consistently paid or not,
it is possible to view Jesus' life, teachings, and healings as

giving permission to the peasants not to pay the temple tax. Such permission would be in service of local rule, local economies, and local access to God's forgiving spirit. Local access to God's forgiveness would have to be understood as an alternative to the pollution system the temple was constructed to address.

The people in the Galilee who heard Jesus teach were most likely small landholders or tenant farmers who feared losing or had lost their land through foreclosure. For these poor agriculturists, access to the temple was a major form of crop insurance. Seeing the temple as the dwelling place of God, and the only place where people could meet God, they perceived the temple and its priests as the mediators of sacrifice and forgiveness.

Since the people of Israel were constituted by God's election, all members of society were considered indebted to God. "Through sacrifice and covenant renewal ceremonies the people accept their debt to Yahweh and discharge their ongoing obligations to him."[18] The only way to discharge their debt was through the temple: by paying the half-shekel tax, by making pilgrimage whenever possible, and by living in obedience to the Torah.

Depending on how the obligation to tithe is interpreted, the effective rate of tribute to the temple was between 13 and 20 percent of a family's annual harvest. On top of the temple tribute were tribute and taxes to Rome and the regional governor, so that subsistence peasants paid between 28 and 40 percent of their stores annually. Landlords and local aristocrats took their additional share through rents, tolls, and other taxes. These multiple mechanisms for extracting wealth from peasants meant that they were always living on the edge.

A central role in redistributing wealth to the landlords was played by the steward, who was entrusted with making contracts and managing the people on the land. The landowners often lived in the cities (or at least had homes in town), engaged in ostentatious consumption, and played politics.[19] Exhortations to become Christian stewards of God's creation are embarrassing in the face of this bit of historical retrieval. The churches have theologized the steward/landlord parables, viewing the landlord as representing God and the steward as representing the rest of us. This is due in large part to the gospelers, who presented the parables of Jesus with their introductory phrases and editorializing final sentences, and in this way construed the received tradition in terms of their own theologies. We may understand the stewardship parables of Jesus more richly if we view the steward as a steward and the landlord as a landlord.

For instance, the parable of the laborers in the vineyard (Matthew 20:1-16) is routinely interpreted as a parable of God's grace that honors no human expectations. When Bill Herzog treats this parable, he recommends that we not include the Matthean introductory formula ("For the reign of heaven is like . . ."), nor the last sentence, a freestanding logion, in a reconstruction of the parable of Jesus. The parable emerges as a device to hold up to Jesus' hearers the scene of hiring day laborers for an amount that is barely a subsistence wage.[20]

> A householder went out early in the morning to hire laborers for his vineyard. After agreeing with the laborers for a denarius a day, he sent them into his vineyard. And going out about the third hour he saw others standing idle in the marketplace; and to them he said, "You go into the vineyard too, and whatever is right I will give you." So they went. Going out again about the sixth hour and the ninth hour, he did the same. And about the eleventh hour he went out and found others standing; and he said to them, "Why do you stand here idle all day?" They said to him, "Because no one has hired us." He said to them, "You go into the vineyard too." And when evening came, the owner of the vineyard said to his steward, "Call the laborers and pay them their wages, beginning with the last, up to the first." And when those hired about the eleventh hour came, each of them received a denarius. Now when the first came, they thought they would receive more; but each of them also received a denarius. And on receiving

it they grumbled at the householder, saying, "These last worked only one hour, and you have made them equal to us who have borne the burden of the day and the scorching heat." But he replied to one of them, "Friend, I am doing you no wrong: did you not agree with me for a denarius? Take what belongs to you, and go; I choose to give to this last as I give to you. Am I not allowed to do what I choose with what belongs to me? Or do you begrudge my generosity?" (Matthew 20:1-16)

These day laborers were probably "excess" children of peasant households who could afford to pass an inheritance to only one child, or they may have been smallholders who lost their land. Day laborers do not get work every day, and the denarius was not sufficient for a sustainable wage. If this society fell true to type of other traditional agrarian societies, the day laborers were in the "expendable" class. All they really owned was their labor, and when through normal attrition they became weak and unable to work, they would beg, as Lazarus did at the gate. And as was the case with Lazarus, begging was followed by death. The vineyard owner, through his steward, paid the last as much as the first and, in so doing, dishonored the labor of the first. Yet at least one spoke up, challenging the vineyard owner's insult. For his effort, he was blacklisted. It may be that Jesus used this parable to promote discussion among his hearers about daily life, their vulnerability in this daily routine, and what the kingdom of God offered in the way of an alternative. What we do not have is access to the way those peasants would have interpreted the kingdom. Perhaps a fair approximation would emerge if we listened in while a farmworker organizer told a similar story to the undocumented day laborers who congregate at the corner of West Francisco and Bellam Avenue, as they do in my region, waiting for day labor.

Another steward parable is found in Luke 16:1-9, the parable of the dishonest steward. It is about an estate manager who faces the prospect of having to become a day laborer and thereby fall into the expendable class.[21]

There was a rich man who had a steward, and charges
were brought to him that this man was wasting his goods.
And he called him and said to him, "What is this that I
hear about you? Turn in the account of your stewardship,
for you can no longer be steward." And the steward said
to himself, "What shall I do, since my master is taking
the stewardship away from me? I am not strong enough
to dig, and I am ashamed to beg. I have decided what
to do, so that people may receive me into their houses
when I am put out of the stewardship." So, summoning
his master's debtors one by one, he said to the first, "How
much do you owe my master?" He said, "A hundred measures of oil." And he said to him, "Take your bill, and sit
down quickly and write fifty." Then he said to another,
"And how much do you owe?" He said, "A hundred measures of wheat." He said to him, "Take your bill, and write
eighty." The master commended the dishonest steward
for his prudence. (Luke 16:1-8)

The verses that follow (vv. 8b-9) seem to be accumulated
sermon notes, and they have complicated the churches' efforts
to understand how this landowner is a representative of God.
Herzog urges, don't even try. The role of the steward was crucial for the landowners, who constituted at most 2 percent of
the population, whereas the peasants constituted 80 percent of
the population. The steward was entrusted with much responsibility, but he was always caught in the crossfire between the
master's greed and the tenants' complaints. Notice that the
steward does not protest his innocence of the charges. He was
guilty of doing his job as the landowner expected. He had
written usurious contracts with hidden interest, and his self-
protective strategy was to decrease the debts by the amount
of interest hidden in the loan. By doing so, he garnered the
debtors' gratitude and the landowner's respect for his shrewd-
ness. Ironically, he became an instrument of a kind of jubilee
(cancellation of debt). The steward saved his skin, and the parable highlights the role of stewards in funneling profits to large
landowners.

For this reason, I hope that we can find other language for talking about ecological responsibility than that of steward-ship. The steward's role in exploitation should not be an anal-ogy for the human relationship with "nature," or with others. Further, it is not good theology to use language that assumes an absentee God.

Considering the multiple mechanisms for extracting wealth from the peasants, it would be understandable if many of them let the temple tax go unpaid. Yet they believed that, if they did not fulfill their obligations to the temple so that the temple could operate on their behalf, the fertility of the land would be jeopardized, they would be permanently indebted, and further, permanently unclean.[22]

In this way, debt was related to impurity. If one was indebted to the temple, one could not present a sin offering to remove impurity and receive forgiveness. Similarly, if one were sick or disabled, as was the paralytic in Mark 2:1-12, one would be unable to go to the temple. Even if one could walk, one would be excluded from temple precincts because of the impurity from illness. Thus, that person would be unable to make the sacrifice to discharge the debt that caused the disability.[23] The story of the paralytic reads as follows:

> When he returned to Capernaum after some days, it was reported that he was at home. So many gathered around that there was no longer room for them, not even in front of the door; and he was speaking the word to them. Then some people came, bringing to him a paralyzed man, car-ried by four of them. And when they could not bring him to Jesus because of the crowd, they removed the roof above him; and after having dug through it, they let down the mat on which the paralytic lay. When Jesus saw their faith, he said to the paralytic, "Son, your sins are forgiven." Now some of the scribes were sitting there, questioning in their hearts, "Why does this fellow speak in this way? It is blasphemy! Who can forgive sins but God alone?" At once Jesus perceived in his spirit that they were discussing these questions among themselves; and he said to them,

"Why do you raise such questions in your hearts? Which is easier, to say to the paralytic, 'Your sins are forgiven,' or to say, 'Stand up and take your mat and walk'? But so that you may know that the Son of Man has authority on earth to forgive sins"—he said to the paralytic—"I say to you, stand up, take your mat and go to your home." And he stood up, and immediately took the mat and went out before all of them; so that they were all amazed and glorified God, saying, "We have never seen anything like this!" (Mark 2:1-12)

Jesus' saying that the man's sins were forgiven, or that his debt was discharged, thus healing the paralytic, was blasphemous to the scribes not because Jesus claimed to do the forgiving. In declaring God's forgiveness, Jesus proposed a strategy of bypassing the temple and establishing another means of access to the forgiving God, that is, through his own mediation. Moreover, if "the son of man" means "an ordinary person," this forgiveness is through the mediation of others.

Jesus Emphasized the Debt Code over the Purity Code

At stake in Jesus' challenge to the scribes is a difference of opinion about where to locate the center of gravity of the Torah itself. There are (at least) two coexisting codes in the Torah, which for the sake of brevity, could be called the debt code and the purity code. In the J and E strands, Yahweh had promised Moses that there would be no more poor in the land if the people would listen to the voice of the Lord and keep the commandments. These included the third-year tithe of produce for the Levites, the sojourners, the fatherless, and the widows within the towns (Deuteronomy 14:28); the sabbatical-year cancellation of debt; and the redistribution of wealth and land in the jubilee year (Deuteronomy 15:4-5). These measures constituted a debt code. They mitigated the power of the elites. This debt-easement legislation was rooted in the oldest traditions of the Hebrew Scriptures.

The instruction regarding how to eliminate pollution constitutes the purity code. It is contained within the Priestly strand (P) of the Torah, and developed after the exile in Babylonia. The Priestly strand took pains to separate the sacred from the profane, the clean from the impure, and the priests from others. This tradition retained the sabbatical and jubilee years but lengthened the period between times of redistribution and shortened the time in between feast days when the priests received sacrifices. Both the debt code and the purity code are evident in Exodus, Leviticus, and Deuteronomy.

A focus on purity codes to avoid the threat of pollution or contagion represented a defense against dissolution into chaos and death. A focus on the debt code represented efforts to avoid the violence that arises when a ruling class exploits the wide base of the population. The debt code provided structures to extend the blessing of the land by sharing it with the Levites, aliens, orphans, and widows, those who otherwise would not have access to the means of production.[24]

These two codes are difficult to maintain in balance. An emphasis on one diminishes the significance of the other. Significant issues take on very different meaning depending on the focus. For instance, poverty interpreted from the point of view of the purity codes is the result of uncleanness. "If one were to respect the quest for purity, one would experience blessing and life."[25] From a focus on the debt-relief legislation, "poverty is the result of covetous greed, which violates the will of Yahweh and compromises the justice of the reign of God."[26]

Jesus seems to have interpreted the Torah's center of gravity to be the debt code. In one of the rare instances in which the Gospels depict him talking to a man of wealth, we read:

> As he was setting out on a journey, a man ran up and knelt before him, and asked him, "Good Teacher, what must I do to inherit eternal life?" Jesus said to him, "Why do you call me good? No one is good but God alone. You know the commandments: 'You shall not murder; You shall not commit adultery; You shall not steal; You shall

not bear false witness; You shall not defraud; Honor your father and mother.'" He said to him, "Teacher, I have kept all these since my youth." Jesus, looking at him, loved him and said, "You lack one thing: Go, sell what you own, and give the money to the poor, and you will have treasure in heaven; then come, follow me." When he heard this, he was shocked and went away grieving, for he had many possessions. (Mark 10:17-22)

If in Jesus' list of commandments, "Do not defraud" is a midrashic expansion of the commandment "do not bear false witness," then in comparison with the version of the the the Decalogue in Exodus 20, Jesus here refers to commandments 5 through 9 and possibly 10. He omits reference to commandments 1 through 4, which refer directly to the honor of God. In Exodus 20, the first commandment is justified by God's bringing the people out of the land of Egypt, the house of slavery. The fourth commandment, to remember the Sabbath, is justified by God's acts of creation and rest thereafter, and the benefits of the Sabbath are for all members of the household, including the other animals, as well as alien residents.[27] God's honor is reflected in God's activity to release those who are bound and to maintain them in social relations of reciprocity and equality.

To have no other gods before Yahweh entails respecting the covenant by respecting Yahweh's gift of the land and, honoring the *principle of extension*, by sharing the gifts with the vulnerable. Observing the wealth of the young man, Jesus suspects that he has another god. In enjoying wealth and intending to inherit it, he has benefited from an exploitative system; he is a social predator who views his wealth as a blessing. The young man believes that he has kept all the commandments because he views them through the lens of the purity code. Jesus, however, views all ten commandments through the lens of the debt code. In order to make the point for the young man, Jesus tells him to go, sell what he has, give it to the destitute, and follow him. The Roman Empire and its client kings and the landed ruling class of Judea (among which was this young man) have subverted the justice of the reign of God.

Through this lens one can read the Sabbath controversies and the healings, where Jesus upstages the scribes and Pharisees in defining who is pure and who is not: he offers God's mercy and forgiveness and declares that the purpose of the Sabbath is to restore life and renew community. Moreover, Jesus intimates that an ordinary layperson can create and change the rules that govern the observance of the Sabbath if that person is mediating God's love, mercy, and forgiveness. The villagers need not funnel their resources to the temple, but can work things out in their own context. The directive to turn the other cheek similarly coaches villagers to avoid appealing to Roman authorities in the event of intra-communal conflict. Rather, they should seek solutions to that conflict within the auspices of the village justice system.

This view of Jesus as a prophet with a political project of creating a community unplugged from the temple emphasizes continuity with the debt-relief measures of the covenants as central to the reign of God. What alternative reign would have given his view any bite?

Herod's son, Herod Antipas, enhancing his father's investment in the Jerusalem temple, built a new capital, Tiberius, on the western shore of the Sea of Galilee, or Kinneret, in 18 C.E. (Jesus was probably born in 4 to 6 B.C.E., so he would have been twenty-two to twenty-four years of age when Tiberius was finished.) To build this city, Herod Antipas populated it with involuntarily displaced peasants, artisans, traders, and foreigners. It was the only Mediterranean port he controlled. He built it as a tourist attraction, to attract travel and business to his territory and to channel travelers to and from Jerusalem.[28]

If Jesus were walking with Mary of Magdala (Magdala being the city with a fishing industry just three miles north of Tiberius) and perhaps Joanna, who was married to one of Antipas's administrative officers, toward the capital, an hour's stroll down the beach would bring them within sight of Antipas's new palace on the cliffside overlooking the sea, the docks, and the freight ships carrying fish products to distant markets. As they drew nearer to the city, they would see the basilica (courthouse) and the other Roman administrative buildings, aqueducts, and theaters. These structures embodied the Roman occupation that was imposed on the land.[29] As a result of these structures and what it took to build and maintain them, Israelite kinship lines and village life were irreparably disrupted by immigration, Hasmonean buyouts of ancestral land, and routine use of rape as a military tactic to terrorize and control people.

Jesus, then, affirmed the survival strategies that people worked out in the midst of empire. He fed the people fish and bread in sufficiency, irrespective of the commodities exchange system, and talked up an alternative *basileia* (kingdom), the *basileia tou theou*, the empire of God. To the question of what he meant by that, I now turn.

CHAPTER SIX

The Reign of God:
Alternative to Empire

Jesus' treatment of the kingdom of God, reign of God, or rule of God might be an important resource for imagining policies to address ecological commitments. This Israelite and Christian symbol is overtly political/economic, in that Galilee and Judea were in fact dominated by the Romans. Thus, the context was the reign of Caesar. If Caesar was not God, then to call for the reign of God was sedition. Since a kingdom is somewhere, the symbol can function at some level to connote place, and places have ecologies. Contemporary New Testament scholars provide consistent (by no means unanimous) evidence that the kingdom of God is at least a central aspect of the teaching of Jesus,[1] if not *the* central element from which every other part of his teaching derives its meaning, and that for Jesus the kingdom challenged the practices and legitimacy of the Roman Empire.

The phrase "kingdom of God" appears infrequently in the Hebrew Scriptures. There are passages in the Hebrew texts that refer to "your kingdom," "my kingdom," "kingship and kingly rule," "Yahweh ruling as king, Yahweh as the eternal king, and Yahweh as the king of the ages. In the Wisdom of Solomon the phrase "the kingdom of God" does occur. The book of Exodus proclaims Yahweh as king because God fought against the Egyptians at the Reed Sea, was victorious for the Israelites, and established the covenant with Israel at Mount Sinai. The book of Psalms contains hymns celebrating Yahweh's kingly rule over creation and Israel, and the book of Isaiah, especially Deutero-Isaiah, out of the despair over the Babylonian exile, speaks of the restoration of God's kingdom in Judah with Jerusalem as its capital. Mention of the restoration and return is found in other prophets, including Jeremiah, Ezekiel, Micah, and others. On a more apocalyptic note, the books of Zechariah and Daniel depict Yahweh as the apocalyptic warrior God winning for his holy city the final world battle. Thus, Jesus had "available" to him a range of symbols connected to the kingdom of God as eternal, as a present reality, or perhaps as a violent world-class confrontation.[2]

The phrase "kingdom of God" appears many times on the lips of Jesus in the Synoptic Gospels, but it appears hardly at all in Paul's epistles, which are nevertheless rather apocalyptic with reference to events surrounding Jesus' second coming. For this reason, the kingdom of God should be distinguished from apocalypticism, though some biblical authors define the two ideas in terms of each other. In any case, it appears that Jesus' usage of the phrase is not traced to its popularity and regular use in either pre-Christian Judaism or first-century Judaism.[3] Jesus seized upon the imagery and language of God's kingly rule and made it a central theme of his own teachings. It was both creative and an appropriation from his tradition.

Whether it was easier for Jesus' hearers to understand what he meant by the kingdom of God than it is for us moderns is not clear. The meaning must not have been all that obvious, considering the number of parables Jesus devoted to the topic. The historical context provided his contemporaries with some cues as to his meaning.

The geographical region of Jesus' life had surely been deeply affected by Herod the Great and the aftermath of his death in 4 B.C.E. After Herod's death, major uprisings erupted in Galilee and Judea. The Roman reconquest of these regions was brutal. In retaliation for the uprising, Roman troops destroyed the city of Sepphoris, just three miles north of Nazareth. The people were enslaved, and many women were raped.[4] Antipas, the son of Herod the Great, inherited the rule of the regions of Galilee and Perea. He rebuilt the city of Sepphoris to be his Galilean capital, a center of Roman political and cultural influence, and hence a focus for the Galileans' resentment. After rebuilding Sepphoris, Antipas built a completely new city, Tiberius, on the shore of the Sea of Galilee (18 B.C.E.). Tiberius was approximately fifteen miles northeast of Nazareth. Antipas mounted this campaign to build two major cities within the first twenty years of his reign. Given that his taxation base was the small producers in villages and towns of Galilee, these two cities would have been a major drain on the economics, culture, and ecology of the Galilean land and people. Yet, strangely, the Gospels and Acts do not mention that Jesus, his disciples, or Paul, Barnabas, and Silas ever set foot in these two cities. The name "Tiberius" actually appears in the Gospel of John, which notes that boats from Tiberius came near where Jesus and the disciples broke bread and ate it and that Jesus and his disciples were by the Sea of Tiberius (Sea of Galilee) (John 6:1, 23; 21:1). But the name otherwise does not appear in the four Gospels. Yet Jesus had a relationship with Mary from Magdala, and Magdala, a major fishery also on the lakeshore, was only three miles north of Tiberius. Many times, Jesus and his disciples were in Capernaum, farther north along the lake, so Tiberius was by no means out of the sphere of their potential travels. I infer that Jesus and his disciples had no base in these centers of Roman influence, and/or refused to develop bases there.

Another part of Jesus' context was the prophet John the Baptist, who became Jesus' mentor sometime around 28 C.E. In the lower Jordan valley, John proclaimed an imminent fiery judgment on Israel. The Baptist offered protection from the coming judgment if people would repent of their sins, reform their lives, and receive a water baptism at his hands. He also referred to the one who was to come, who would baptize with the Holy Spirit instead of water. Jesus, apparently seeing himself as needing to repent and reform, sought baptism from John. He may have stayed for a while as one of John's disciples to perform an apprenticeship. But at some point Jesus began his own public ministry, distinguishing his message from John's at certain points, though sharing with John the sense of imminent judgment. Unique to Jesus was the message that God was to come in power to save God's people and to heal and restore them.[5] In the context of colonization by the Roman Empire, such an alternative rule would be good news indeed. Jesus also offered his healing ministry and exorcisms as a present embodiment of the kingdom about to come.

In addition to John the Baptist, another part of the historical context for Jesus' generation, and those immediately after the Gospels were composed, were several popular messianic movements, led by figures recognized as kings by both their followers and the empire, leaders who succeeded in ruling certain areas of the country for a time. These kings and their movements appear to stand in, or to be a revival of, an ancient Israelite tradition of popularly elected, and thus anointed, accountable, conditional, and covenanted leadership. David was such an anointed king; later David was "decommissioned" and Absalom was anointed. According to the historian Josephus, during Jesus' era and that of the gospelers, the kings and their movements were particularly significant at two specific times: one was during the popular uprising following the death of Herod (4 C.E.), and the second was during the Great Revolt against Rome (66–70 C.E.)[6]

In 4 C.E., Simon, the former Herodian servant Anthronges, and Judas, son of Ezekias, either claimed the kingship or were acclaimed as king. Their followers were largely from the peasantry, and the goals of their movements were to achieve liberation from Herodian-Roman domination and to reestablish a more egalitarian social structure in line with their perception of God's will. They were able to take control of areas within their respective districts of Galilee, Perea, and Judea. It took a sizable military force for the Romans to reclaim these territories, making a big impact on towns and villages in the geographical location where Jesus was born, and within a few years of Jesus' birth. It was only a few miles north of Nazareth where the town of Sepphoris was burned and its inhabitants sold into slavery.[7]

Simon bar Giora and Menahem were significant leaders who marshaled resistance against Rome during the Great Revolt. Menahem and his followers went to the temple and burned the public archives, to, according to Josephus, destroy the moneylenders' bonds and prevent the recovery of debts, in order to cause a rising of the poor against the rich. Simon bar Giora was the principal political-military commander in Jerusalem while it was under Roman siege, followed as king by thousands of people and a sizable army. This movement also sought to achieve military organization and preparation for a prolonged war of resistance and to restore social and economic justice, which they saw as God's will. When Simon bar Giora surrendered to the Roman army, he did so as "King of the Jews."[8]

Richard Horsley comments on the significance of these messianic movements' capacities to maintain popular sovereignty and independence for periods ranging from a few weeks to a few years, built as they were on the peasantry's honored tradition of anointing their king to lead them in liberation, and their capacities for taking collective action. I am struck by the actual hopes of the people, not only for an accountable leader but also for a just political/social order that they perceived to be God's will.

With this context for the ministry and teaching, or community organizing, of Jesus of Nazareth, it can be said that the kingdom of God was an alternative to and a criticism of the Roman Empire. Jesus spoke of the kingdom as something that would come in the future, for example, in the Lord's Prayer (Matthew 6:9-13; Luke 11:2-4), in which he prays, "Come, Father, to rule as king"; and in the Beatitudes, "Happy are the poor, for theirs is the kingdom of heaven. Happy are the mourners, for they shall be comforted. Happy are the hungry, for they shall be satisfied."

But he also spoke of the kingdom as already present in his ministry. "If by the finger of God I cast out the demons, then the kingdom of God has come upon you" (Matthew 12:28; Luke 11:20). "Can the wedding guests fast when the bridegroom is with them?" (Mark 2:18-20). Stories of Jesus' healing of the blind, of those who could not walk, and of lepers stood along-side his exorcisms as manifestations of God's rule. The accounts of Jesus by the gospelers present him as using both the future tense and the present tense to describe the kingdom of God.

But Mark, Luke, Matthew, and John (all of whom wrote after the destruction of the temple by Rome during the Great Revolt and knew of the Roman reconquest) spiritualized the concept of the kingdom, divesting the term of any specific political content.[9] After Jesus' resurrection, the apostles took his message to the synagogues of Judea and to the Diaspora. Those who received the apostles' message—Galileans, Judeans, and some Gentiles—formed or joined an *ekklēsia* within the synagogue. But after fifty years, when Jesus had not returned, the kingdom was delayed, and the Romans still occupied the land, the movement was predominantly Gentile. Paula Fredriksen, trying to recapture the social psychology of the period, appraises: "Too many Gentiles, too few Jews, and no End in sight."[10] Within 150 years the church would regard Jewish Christians as heretics.[11] What started as a Jewish reform movement developed into "Christianity" and became anti-Jewish.[12]

A consensus seems to have formed that the Gospels did not perceive the kingdom solely in apocalyptic terms. As much or as little as Jesus waited on God to create a cataclysmic overturning of history, he also saw the kingdom as a pattern of relations that were possible, feasible, and actionable among the Galilean peasants of that day. And the negative consequences for today's churches of overemphasizing the future (eschatological) and particularly the apocalyptic version of the kingdom of God, reach beyond failure to grasp the truth of the moral valence of the kingdom for Jesus.[13] If the person and significance of Jesus of Nazareth must be linked by faith to a cosmic battle against the forces of evil, and the end of history, then such a faith for its vindication is necessarily tied to the destruction of the earth. For those who view the world through religiously affected lenses—and probably most do—even apparently secular, earth-threatening phenomena may take on an aura of religious inevitability if deity-sponsored apocalyptic is a sign of any kind of "salvation."[14] What possible definition of salvation is at play in the headlong rush into human-induced biocide?

I recommend that we be agnostic about whether a battle between the cosmic forces of good and evil is in God's plan for the universe, born as it was billions of years ago out of God's creative love. The moral dimension of the Christian life should focus instead on what we do have control over.[15] The kingdom of God signifies in Jesus' teachings a just social order, defined differently perhaps from culture to culture, because it is dependent in some sense on the situation of injustice it is to address. But in all cases it is a "proposal" to distribute the benefits of social/economic life together so that all are sustained, including plants and animals. Moreover, it is a challenge to the contemporary order, which fails to sustain the base of the population and the web of creation to which it is tied. We can continue Jesus' project in the present with integrity.

Marianne Sawicki has another way of saying this: "The Kingdom of God is not free-standing. It has to be sought in the midst of something else."[16] Jesus was standing on land that was ruled by the Romans through Herod Antipas. Clearly, the kingdom of God did not refer to Roman rule. The empire of God would do the same sorts of things that the Roman administration did, "but would do them in favor of the people of the land rather than for the benefit of the colonizers and their clients."[17]

God's basilica, unlike the basilica in Tiberius, would dispense justice: it would manage the distribution of food and other commodities, return tithes and tolls to the local economy, and bring people together in new affinities, apart from traditional kinship lines. It would not govern through the reckoning of purity or tithing, and in this way would be independent of the temple. Nor would it be enclosed in a built environment—Jesus dispensed free food on the lakeshore (wild water rather than aqueduct water) in open air.

Roman occupation was an affront to the Galilean indigenous cultural perception of how humankind was to relate to God's purposes. Rome used its roads, seaports, urban buildings, and basilica to enforce its empire. The *basileia* of Rome disrupted nearly every material expression of divine sovereignty. But to the people of the land, it is God who really governs. God's empire is in our midst, no matter what we do for or against it.

> You won't be able to observe the coming of God's *basilea*. People are not going to be able to say, "Look, here it is!" or "Over there!" On the contrary, God's basilea is right there in your presence. (Luke 17:20-21)

Human beings either hinder God's natural processes and human relationships or help them. Humankind cooperates with divine rule when we intervene to adjust the universe at times of decision, or whenever things or people have gotten off track. Our capacity, and thereby the invitation God extends to us, is to "assist in channeling and correcting the flow of real relationships."[18] The indigenous worldview attempted to align human activities with the Creator's intentions, rather than dominate nature preeminently for human consumption.

Yet another lens through which to look at the kingdom of God is that of Antoinette Clark Wire, who believes that when *basileia* is translated as "kingdom," or even "empire," moderns cannot grasp what first-century people in Palestine would understand. Her translation of the word is "inheritance." God's kingdom indeed challenges the rule of domination. But it does not therefore refer to God's own rule or judging. It is a bestowing of sovereignty or independence upon a people. God's legacy to us is to give us a chance to use our freedom to construct the justice and peace that we need as a people.[19]

> By saying God's inheritance is theirs, Jesus assures the poor that the land or resources necessary for common livelihood and independence belong to them and to all who are incorporated into the family line of the prophets by their poverty or abuse.[20]

This use of the term *inheritance* does not have the individualistic meaning that we usually associate with inheritance. People who come from a culture of communal ownership will relate to this meaning of inheritance. The rich young man of Mark 10 had a difficult time inheriting "eternal life" because he was in line to inherit family wealth, an inheritance he did not want to forgo. On the other hand, God's inheritance is for sustaining the community as a whole, including the weak and vulnerable within it. Whenever tempted to use "kingdom of God," try substituting the term "inheritance of God."

In the period following Herod's death, there were brutal suppressions using mass crucifixions of popular prophets of justice and their followers, and again during the Jewish Revolt of 66–70 (the latter period would not have affected Jesus' views, but it would have made a big impression on Mark, Matthew, Luke, and John). These events contributed to an apocalyptic fervor in the Galilee and Judea in the first century.[21] This apocalypticism appears in the Gospels and in Paul's letters in different ways and with different degrees of urgency. In Paul's letters especially, the kingdom of God signified the end of history. Jesus would come again as the Christ, the Mighty Warrior and at the same time the Prince of Peace, accompanied by great displays of power,.

For many Christians today, it is troubling to define the reign of God in historical terms as a reality that we have some responsibility to nurture. They believe that the kingdom of God is what Jesus Christ will usher in, and it seems presumptuous to take any responsibility for it at all. To see the image of the kingdom of God as a result of divine intervention "somewhere else" or at the "end of time" reflects apocalyptic language, but it may not have been Jesus' teaching. I use the growth parables in Mark as an indication that what Jesus taught about the reign of God can be characterized as a restoration of righteousness, consistent with Isaiah 11.[22] Similar to other restoration passages in the Hebrew Scriptures, the growth parables point to the intrinsic relationship between the righteous rule of God, the processes of nature, and human life.[23] In this way the parables provide an alternative vision of our inheritance to that of apocalypticism.

> Listen! A sower went out to sow. And as he sowed, some seed fell on the path, and the birds came and ate it up. Other seed fell on rocky ground, where it did not have much soil, and it sprang up quickly, since it had no depth of soil. And when the sun rose, it was scorched; and since it had no root, it withered away. Other seed fell among thorns, and the thorns grew up and choked it, and it yielded no grain. Other seed fell into good soil and brought forth grain, growing up and increasing and yielding thirty and sixty and a hundredfold. (Mark 4:3-8)

When Jesus told this and other parables to the peasants, he was holding up a picture of their life to them, introducing something surprising into it, and posing an opportunity for them to discuss what life was like for them and how it could be different. What would the peasants listening have heard in this parable? Given the hard-packed earth of the path, the thin soil of the rocky area, and the thorns typical of impoverished soil, this smallholder or lease holder was probably coping with pressures to grow crops on land that was not good or had been overworked. But some good soil was present. The nonirrigated farmland in Mediterranean climate of wet season and dry season could perhaps at best yield five times the seed planted. But this harvest yielded thirty- sixty- and a hundredfold. The reign of God would be different from the reign of the Romans and the landlords. The efforts of the people of the soil would be rewarded generously. They would have a large harvest—one that they could eat. Later in the same chapter of Mark, we read:

> He also said, "The Kingdom of God is as if someone would scatter seed on the ground, and would sleep and rise night and day, and the seed would sprout and grow, he does not know how. The earth produces of itself, first the stalk, then the head, then the full grain in the head. But when the grain is ripe, at once he goes in with his sickle, because the harvest has come." (Mark 4:26-29)

The soil produces on its own. The earth nourishes growth by processes that humans witness, prepare for, but do not always understand. This parable underscores an element of mystery, as nature's action in growing the seed into a harvest happens while the farmer sleeps. Yet if natural processes are ongoing without human aid, it is human cooperation with nature that ensures a plentiful harvest. Social practices and relations of expropriation can result in the plunder of the earth. But if we acknowledge the processes of nature and cooperate with them, we are assured of plenty.[24]

This parable may reflect Jesus' effort to drive a wedge between the temple and the land. The land produces of itself; it does not depend on sacrifices.[25] But we should not miss an important feature of this parable—there is no cultivation, no toil. Peasants in first-century Palestine had a life analogous to black sharecroppers in the Mississippi Delta after emancipation, whose labor was hard and long, and they never were able to make enough on their harvests to pay off the debt to the white landowner. In Jesus' day, too, peasants' labor was hard and long, and they were working to pay tribute to Rome, tribute to the regional governor, and rent to the landowner; to save enough back for the next year's planting; to pay the tithe to the temple; and to have food for the animals and the whole family. Their toil was overwhelmingly for someone else. The reign of God was not to leave the land. It was to live with the fruit of the land without the backbreaking toil for someone else.

In the next verses we read:

He also said, "With what can we compare the kingdom of God, or what parable will we use for it? It is like a mustard seed, which, when sown upon the ground, is the smallest of all the seeds on earth; yet when it is sown it grows up and becomes the greatest of all shrubs, and puts forth large branches, so that the birds of the air can make nests in its shade." (Mark 4:30-32)

Mustard was a condiment cultivated in Galilean gardens, but wild mustard was a common weed. Because the seeds were small and the plant produced them quickly, this plant would be difficult to eradicate from one's soil after one specimen made its appearance. In this parable, however, there is appreciation for the mustard plant, not because of its usefulness for the farmer but because in the web of life it provided protection for wild birds. The reign of God is not only for humankind; it is also for wild kind. On this earth.

In this way of reading the parables of Jesus, we get an earthy perspective. The parables were spoken to people of the land who knew what it meant to try to grow crops on poor land or good. These words were spoken to a people for whom the land was a special link in their relationship with God, but they had witnessed the land coming increasingly under the control of a few absentee owners. The parables pointed to a social order that would not exploit those who worked the land and that would acknowledge the place for wild nature. But overwhelmingly, the kingdom of God, the inheritance of God, was a historical project, concerned about the affairs of nature. Thus, we see in these parables the sense of the divineness of the natural world.

I conclude that the politics of Jesus, consistent with his Galilean heritage, was to qualify the tie between the villages and the temple in Jerusalem. The qualification he modeled meant sidestepping, or stepping aside from, the temple and the priests in everyday village life. Instead, he nourished the social capital that was necessary to sustain the people in small communities, bearing up under foreign domination but embedded in their ecologies.

CHAPTER SEVEN

Paul's Challenge to Caesar

Just as the depiction of the historical context of Galilee and Judea during the first century B.C.E. and C.E. affects the way we interpret the significance of the Gospels as resources for the contemporary situation, so also with Paul's letters.

It is not only possible, but necessary, according to the biblical research I am about to harvest, to read the letters of Paul in a manner that reveals his attitudes toward social, political, and economic structures. The base line is his resistance to the Roman Empire. As is true for the Gospels, the context of Paul's letters includes mechanisms the Romans used to consolidate their power over a far-flung geographic area. Although military conquest institutionalizing slavery, taxation, and extraction of resources was certainly the first mechanism to add territory and wealth to the empire, the Romans relied on more subtle means to sustain their power, including the memory of their past pillage, murder, enslavement, and the threat of using military force in the future.[1] Selective execution by public crucifixion was one of the mechanisms for inducing fear in the population. Yet the rhetoric of peace and concord extolling the salvific policies of Caesar was fostered in civic life, at the same time that the avenues for democratic participation were impaired. A system of patronage organized social relations from the base of the population to local and regional elites to the emperor, and elites marked their power through their capacity for philanthropy, creating a chain of asymmetrical and hierarchical power. Finally, a cult of the emperor, fostered by local elites, reached enormous proportions during the reign of Caesar Augustus (d. 6 C.E.), but it lasted through mid-first century. Augustus and the following Caesars were trumpeted as sent by providence as saviors, putting an end to war. In gratitude to Caesar "for bringing the breath of life for all and establishing the common good," cities, through decisions of their councils and their populace, vied with one another to accumulate funds for festivals; to build temples to the "God" or "son of God," Augustus; to organize games; and to conduct regular cycles of celebrations, called "the imperial days."[2] The regularity of such festivals focusing on the emperor god reinforced the perception among the populace that the Roman Empire was stable and permanent, and also that the emperor was present to people far and wide simultaneously.[3]

Against this backdrop, Paul wrote several letters to *ekklēsiai* ("assemblies"), encouraging them in the faith, using what authority he had to influence their dynamics and practices, and reminding them of the cosmic consequences of their living enriched by God's Holy Spirit and the phenomena it stimulated in them. Of special note for our purposes is a section in his Letter to the Romans, in which appear these words:

> For the creation waits with eager longing for the revealing of the children of God; for the creation was subjected to futility, not of its own will but by the will of the one who subjected it, in hope that the creation itself will be set free from its bondage to decay and will obtain the freedom of the glory of the children of God. We know

that the whole creation has been groaning in labor pains until now; and not only the creation, but we ourselves, who have the first fruits of the Spirit, groan inwardly while we wait for adoption, the redemption of our bodies. (Romans 8:19-30)

This section in its entirety makes explicit that the consequences of redemption (restored honor) at the Messiah's hand were to benefit the people of Israel but also all of creation. According to first-century Mediterranean beliefs, all of creation included celestial, terrestrial, and human entities, all of which spheres exerted mutual influence and impact on one another.[4] God's creation has been subject to sin because of humans. But with the "revealing of the children of God" ("revealing" being a translation of a word meaning the "apocalypse"), there will be cosmic repercussions. "God's raising Jesus indicates an end to death, both for those who have faith in God and . . . for all creation who will share in some way in that faith."[5]

One would expect, then, that the apostle Paul would offer perspectives that would be relevant to the question of how to reflect on climate change policies. He at least acknowledged the impact of human "sin" on the rest of creation. But what in Paul's work shapes the way faithful people address the sin that has been affecting creation? The interpreter of his letters has a few tasks to accomplish before a view of Paul's relevance for our purposes can emerge. One of those tasks is to determine which of the letters attributed to Paul were probably written by him and which were written in his name by someone else later. No consensus about this matter can be firmly established, in large part because of the theological presuppositions regarding the "literal" truth of the collected works in the New Testament, and whether tradition criticism, source criticism, or textual criticism are legitimate. The scholars whom I consulted for this section reflect a kind of consensus that the *undisputed letters of Paul*, written between 49 or 50 C.E. and through the 50s, are 1 Thessalonians (written first), 1 Corinthians, 2 Corinthians, Philippians, Philemon, Galatians, and Romans (written last? or perhaps Philemon was written last). *Students/disciples of Paul*, an "early Pauline school," wrote (between 70 and 90 C.E.) 2 Thessalonians, Colossians, and Ephesians. Finally, a *later Pauline school* (between 100 and 125 C.E.) wrote 1 Timothy, 2 Timothy, and Titus.

Neil Elliott further proposes:[6]

- The verses pronouncing God's judgment upon "the Jews who killed Jesus" (1 Thessalonians 2:14-16) or commanding women to silence (1 Corinthians 14:34-35) are interpolations, or additions, edited into Paul's genuine letters after the apostle's death.[7]

- A significant minority of scholars contend that the command to submit to governments (Romans 13:1-7) is also a late interpolation, but the evidence of interference of manuscript copyists is not present as it was in the manuscripts of 1 Thessalonians and 1 Corinthians. Therefore, the interpretation of Romans 13:1-7 must be informed by the history of attacks on Jewish communities in the Diaspora and Paul's perception that governmental protection was necessary for the survival of (developing) Judaism.[8]

The letters collected in the New Testament that are falsely attributed to Paul are called "pseudepigrapha," or "deutero-Pauline." They present an interesting challenge to readers of the text because they were written in the name of Paul by others, deliberately altering the received tradition. They are forgeries.[9] They are significant, however, because of the filtering effect they have had on our reading of the authentic letters of Paul. Biblical commentaries through the centuries have interpreted Paul through the lens of (pseudo) "Paul." The effect is to complicate the readers' capacities to imagine the other voices in the assemblies, the *ekklēsiai*, to whom Paul was responding, and whom he was seeking to influence. On the basis of the politics in the pseudepigraphical letters, it appears that the early *ekklēsiai* were conflicted about how to interpret Paul's letters. We can surmise that the conflict had something to do with gender in the *ekklēsia*, and also with the significance of baptism for the status of slaves, because perspectives on these issues appear in the forged letters. But we do not know who held the rival interpretations and what their views were.[10] It is still possible to see reflected in Paul's letters and the book of Acts:

> women were among the most prominent missionaries and leaders in the early Christian movement. They were apostles and ministers like Paul, and some were his co-workers. They were teachers, preachers, and competitors in the race for the gospel. They founded house churches and, as prominent patrons, used their influence for other missionaries and Christians.[11]

With regard to the status of slaves, the forged letters contained appeals to slaves to be obedient to their masters. If these letters are removed from the table for purposes of understanding Paul's politics, two passages in his authentic letters remain regarding slavery: 1 Corinthians 7:21 and the letter to the house church that includes Philemon, the owner of the slave Onesimus. With respect to the Corinthian passage, because most translations have rendered this sentence as, "Even if you have the opportunity to become free, make use of your slavery instead," Paul has been vulnerable to the charge of having a conservative social ethic. But this translation requires awkward syntax, and throughout 1 Corinthians 7 Paul repeatedly allows that Christians may change their status without sinning. The better translation would be, "If you have the opportunity to become free, by all means take it."[12] But when Paul's voice is filtered through the pseudo-Pauline letters, particularly the "station in life" translations of Colossians 3:18—4:1; Ephesians 5:22—6:9; and 1 Timothy 2:8-15 and 6:1-2, his perspective appears more quietistic, conservative, and reluctant to challenge social structures.

In the letter to the house church in which Philemon was participating, Paul appeals for Onesimus, a slave (?), and perhaps one who has escaped, to be accepted back as a brother. He does not challenge the institution of slavery directly. Yet it would be difficult to mesh Onesimus's status as brother with another status as slave.[13] Moreover, nowhere in this letter does the reader find any reference to the slave's obedience. Rather, the appeal is to the master to be obedient instead.[14]

There remains the advice to the Romans (13:1-6) that every person be subject to governing authorities, for there is no authority except from God. The "modern" reader will have to keep in mind the Roman emperor's practice of ruling through local elites and the practices involved in the patronage system, whereby positions of civic authority were obtained in a variety of ways by persons who likely were large landowners in the region and had been most effective not only in supporting the flow of resources to the empire but also in maintaining a certain peacefulness in this flow. The Jesus group members to whom Paul wrote might well have been resident foreigners or resident aliens—therefore, not citizens (persons with rights in the city). If so, their vulnerability would have been a significant factor in Paul's admonition to be subject to governing authorities.[15]

The question of the authenticity of Paul's authorship concerns which texts serve as determinative for understanding his views of social organization, which in turn will have bearing on whether and in what ways we can use the letters of Paul as a resource for our perspectives on climate change policies. The issue involves several background discussions of matters concerning which we will not be able to make strong claims: Why do we care whether Paul wrote these letters? How do we know that the other authors were not writing out of more "justifiable" stances than Paul's position? Are we attempting to identify a canon within the canon that is purer, truer, and more compelling than other texts? If so, why do that? In my view, it is because some church traditions hold that the letters of Paul are truly the heart of the New Testament, more significant than the Gospels for understanding the core matters of the Christian faith. Thus, the effort to discuss whether to harvest from

Paul's letters is worth some discussion. In this light, I will try to represent in a basic way some efforts by biblical scholars to show that Paul did have an agenda that undergirded his missionary efforts, and that agenda was a serious challenge to the authority of the Roman emperor:

Paul's Focus on the Cross of Christ Is Intrinsically Political

Neil Elliott makes the case that Paul, by making the crucifixion of Jesus central to his message, tapped into the history of the Roman use of crucifixion as a deterrent to popular rebellion and acknowledged people's fears of Roman terrorism, but trumped that reign of terror by preaching the resurrection of God's Son as a sign of the imminent apocalypse. "Acts of exemplary violence such as crucifixion make large-scale social control possible."[16] But the murder of Jesus shows only the power of state violence and the power of the policies of the empire to violate the web of all creation (Romans 8:22-23). Jesus' death is the beginning of God's final war against all such oppressive political power. But it is just the beginning. The rulers of this age are not yet overcome (contra Colossians 2:15). The people of God are called to "live in the Spirit," and they groan in sympathy with the rest of oppressed creation, resisting the efforts of the pagan empire to rule in God's place.[17]

The death of Jesus was not a sacrifice demanded by God; it was an act of political suppression of the Romans. The earliest Jesus movement groups did not see the death of Jesus in cultic terms as atonement for sins of others.[18] This idea took root in later interpretations, possibly influenced by the logic of blood cults in the larger social environment, but reflected nevertheless in the New Testament in the Letter to the Hebrews. Paul's own letters show that he recognized a tendency to such logic and opposed it.[19]

Paul Challenged the Emperor by Organizing *Ekklēsiai* as an Alternative to Roman Rule

The term *ekklēsia* in the Greek-speaking eastern Roman Empire designated the citizen "assembly" of the Greek polis. It was a "democratic congress" of full decision-making citizens.[20] The translation of *ekklēsia* as "church" is anachronistic. Though *ekklēsiai* in which Paul participated, and which he influenced, did involve praise, acclamation, and discussion of issues of concern to the citizenry, so also did the other assemblies in the Greek polis referred to as *ekklēsiai*.[21] In this respect the *ekklēsiai* can be described as local communities alternative to the Roman order, in competition with the official city assembly.[22] They were emancipatory projects in this sense: there is some basis for believing that the praxis of the *ekklēsiai* involved collectively purchasing the freedom of enslaved members, organizing the collection for the saints in Jerusalem as a practice of solidarity, and instilling within each person that she or he is the agent of change, and not merely the recipient of justice.[23]

Paul's Missionary Efforts Were Necessary in His Eyes to Bring to Fulfillment the Restoration Envisioned in Isaiah 11:10 and Psalm 117:1

The *ekklēsiai*, or assemblies, were scattered women and men loyal to Jesus as lord, "forming colonial outposts of the empire that is to be." From Caesar's point of view they were subversive, but the texts of the "Israelites" foretold a time when the earth would be filled with the glory of the God of Abraham and when the nations would join Israel in singing God's praises.[24] The God of Israel promised deliverance from oppression for the children of Israel but also for all the peoples of the world.[25] The *ekklēsiai* were the foretaste of that deliverance and evidence that such deliverance was about to occur.

Paul's Missionary Efforts Were Authorized by the Delivery of the "Collection"

The collection for the saints in Jerusalem is described in Galatians 2:1-10 as rooted in the meeting in Jerusalem where James, Peter, and John agreed that Paul and Barnabas could orient their mission to the uncircumcised.[26] It is in this account that Paul says, "They asked only one thing, that we remember the poor, which was actually what I was eager to do." Concern for the poor does not receive attention in the other references Paul makes regarding the collection (Romans 15:25-28; 1 Corinthians 16:1-4; 2 Corinthians 8–9; Galatians 2:10), but he was very concerned to follow through with the collection.[27]

Although collection of the temple tax was a long-standing practice of the Judeans and those in the Diaspora, a few people believe that the collection to which the Letter to the Galatians refers was Paul's innovation. Allen Dwight Callahan refers to it as an instance of "international economic reciprocity."[28] Richard Horsley describes it as an outgrowth of a network of assemblies with an international political-economic dimension opposed to the tributary political economy of the empire.[29] Sze-kar Wan's analysis is that the collection is Paul's effort to redefine group boundaries to include Gentile converts, consistent with the "universalism" evident in Isaiah 2:2-3; 60:4-7; 61:6; and Micah 4:1-2. In these texts, the in-breaking of the eschatological age, "the end time," is evidenced by all the nations streaming to the mountain of the Lord, on which is the house of God, in Jerusalem. The nations will bring their wealth and will praise the Lord. And God will teach all the nations the ways of political peace and economic justice.[30] So the collection was of great concern to Paul because it was another functional sign of God's great intervention to destroy the empire of the false god. This vision is of course political. It proclaims the sovereignty of God over all the nations, a clear alternative to one of the Caesars. Not Rome, but Jerusalem, will be the capital.

Paul Challenged the Patronage System

Paul made efforts to raise the collection around Asia Minor, Macedonia, and Greece. The multilateral quality of the collection had political significance. It challenged the vertical organization of power of the patronage system, wherein a patron expends on a client, creating a bond of gratitude and indebtedness and assigning superiority/inferiority statuses to all participants in the structure. Since the collection was gathered from multiple sources, the patronal dynamic that potentially would affect the Jerusalem assembly in nonreciprocal power dynamics was blunted. In 2 Corinthians 8–9, Paul reminds the Corinthians of the Macedonian contributions, thereby lowering the patronal dynamic of the Corinthians' gift. Likewise, when Paul points to God as the source of all wealth, and when he refused to accept money from the Corinthian congregation, he undercut the patronal dynamic.[31]

I am convinced that Paul's letters can and should be interpreted in light of this awareness of the political situation. Dieter Georgi punctuates the necessity for a political lens by reminding us that Paul was probably a prisoner himself when he came to Rome—and in Rome he was tried and executed. He reads Acts 28:30-31 and *1 Clement* 5 to indicate that both Paul and Peter were charged and convicted independently of, and probably before, the persecution ordered by Nero (emperor 54 to 68 C.E.).[32] The picture that comes through most clearly is that Paul was subversive because he challenged the ideology of Rome's universal and benevolent rule, and the way he did that was consistent with Isaiah's challenge to the Babylonian cult and Deuteronomy's rejection of all paganism in favor of the creator and covenant God.[33] Yet it is easier for me to hear his "anti-speech" than his strategic and sociological vision. N. T. Wright poses the question, "If Paul's answer to Caesar's empire is the empire of Jesus, what does that say about this new empire, living under the rule of its new Lord?"[34] This is an excellent way of formulating the question in which I am interested, but Wright goes on to answer the question theologically, only indirectly implying sociology or economics. Perhaps most of the authors in this vein could also say that it is difficult to make positive statements about the alternative political and social organization that would flow from Paul's critical stance against the pagan worship of Caesar. Further work is in order to see if this issue can be clarified.

In the dialogue stimulated by this effort to expose the effect of empire on the New Testament, complicating interpretations of Paul's ministry have been articulated. They share with the foregoing authors the commitment to expose the effect of the Roman Empire on any effort to exegete Paul's letters. Further, they raise serious and interesting questions that, if valid, significantly undermine the usefulness of Paul's letters for our purposes.

How Can Paul's Relationships to the *Ekklēsiai* be Alternatives to the Roman Empire in Light of His Efforts to Limit the Influence of Women?

The baptismal formula to which Paul refers in Galatians 3:28 had the effect of abolishing status differentials: in Christ there is neither Judean nor Greek, no longer slave or free, no longer male and female. This formula antedated Paul and expressed the early Jesus movement's sense that all are created in God's image, consistent with the creation story of Genesis 1:27. The *ekklēsiai* were baptizing women and slaves, whether or not the husband/father/master was also baptized. To include in the assemblies people who would be subordinates in the patriarchal household represented a significant challenge to the organization of society, in which the family was considered a unit of the state and the paradigm for the state.[35]

Yet it is difficult to know whether Paul supported this egalitarian ethos or compromised it. He uses the formula in Galatians, and quotes it in 1 Corinthians 12:13 (but there he does not mention the third pair, "male and female"). His discussion of why women should cover their heads while praying and prophesying (1 Corinthians 11:2-16) seems important to him and conveys a hierarchical hand. Further in this letter, 14:33b-36 (which may have been inserted by a later writer, but may represent Paul's own view) states that women should be silent in the churches and should be subordinate, waiting until arriving home to ask their husbands questions about what was said or done. Segments of the historical Christian churches cling to the view that these are Paul's words, and *because* they are, women's active participation in and leadership of worship should be limited, hardly the basis for a radical challenge to Roman or any other patriarchal, hierarchal power structure.

Antoinette Clark Wire believes that there is a basis for holding that verses 33b-36 do constitute Paul's position. She proposes that Paul should be viewed as someone losing status while the Corinthian women prophets were experiencing rising social importance as members of the assembly at Corinth. She identifies six social markers in Paul's own writing: wisdom, power, family name or honor, ethnic group, condition of servitude, and gender.[36] Paul, before joining the Jesus movement, would have had high social status in this regard:

> [H]e comes from a Hellenistic Jewish family with the wealth to foster a son's education and with political influence used in Rome's favor to win citizenship. Paul is also favored in the other three status indicators—Jew, free, and male. . . . In wisdom, power, rank, ethnic security, caste, and sex, Saul—to use Luke's name for him at this stage—has status.[37]

By entering the mission to the "Gentiles," Paul's position among the Pharisees seemingly would have been compromised. He admits to the Corinthians that he has not spoken wisdom. His honor in that assembly would therefore have been compromised. His ethnic identity, caste, and gender (Jew, free, and male) would have remained sources of status, and in relation to the women he would have higher status overall. But in relation to his prior social identity, he would have suffered loss, a chosen loss, and one that would ready him for identifying with the crucified Christ.

But the women in Corinth, like others who were once
without status, rose in status upon being accepted into the
ekklēsia and especially when they received the gifts of the
spirit of glossolalia and prophecy, gifts that were not limited
to people who in the eyes of the dominant society were of
high status. The women, once ignorant, weak, and shamed had
become strong, wise, and honored.[38] They had experienced
new freedom in God's Spirit, and had experienced such freedom directly, unmediated by the men in the assembly. Their
gain in status seems to be mirrored in their view of the power
of the risen Christ to give them such new life and freedom. If
Paul is standing on the down escalator, preaching Christ crucified, he meets the women in Corinth as they are rising up
on the escalator's other side, prophesying and speaking with
tongues of angels, rejoicing in the power of the Holy Spirit to
affect their lives.[39]

How Can Paul Challenge the Political Authority of the Lord and Savior Caesar While Establishing His Own Position in an Alternative Hierarchical Order?

In the first letter to the Corinthians appear several implied
hierarchies (1 Corinthians 3:22 = you–Christ–God; 4:14 =
children–father–in Christ; and 11:13 = woman–man–Christ–
God). Building on Wire's work in *Corinthian Women Prophets,*
Cynthia Briggs Kittredge proposes that "God's subjection of
Christ is the ultimate symbolic legitimization of the father's
position between the children and Christ and the husband's
position between his wife and God."[40] These linked hierarchical relationships resemble the patronage system that integrated
the Roman Empire. In 1 Corinthians 12, concerning "spiritual
gifts," Paul acknowledges that there are a variety of gifts, but
their origin is the same Spirit. To each is given the manifesta-
tion of the Spirit for the common good. He uses the body as
the metaphor, making the case that all parts of the body are
necessary, and likening the *ekklēsia* in Corinth to the body of
Christ. Then he introduces the hierarchy of gifts, privileging

the "apostles," of which he maintains he is one (12:28). Finally, he encourages the Corinthians to strive for the greater gifts, and he, Paul, will show them a still more excellent way.

Wire says, "It is not clear how Paul can call people to seek certain gifts above others, since he has just argued that gifts are distributed "as the spirit wills" or "as God chose" (12:11, 18). But Paul goes on to attempt to harness the practices of prophesying to the standard of love, life for the good of others (13:4-7). Wire suggests that the women prophets of Corinth were seeking to realize a different social practice. "Their watchword is probably not 'love,' which calls for self-sacrifice from a position of advantage, but more likely 'spirit' or 'wisdom' (14:37; 3:18), signifying a power divinely kindled among once inert people."[41]

The passage about the silencing of the women appears in 1 Corinthians 14:34-36, and there is enough dispute concerning the authorship of it that the New Revised Standard Version puts these verses in parentheses, acknowledging the question. But Wire calls our attention to the verses immediately following, in which Paul drops all other forms of appeal and picks up the claim that what he is saying is the command of the Lord, as though he needs to stonewall because he will get no further with rational appeals. Apparently the women's speech in Corinth's *ekklēsia* is "the heart of the alternative spiritual authority to his own."[42] The First Letter to the Corinthians is loaded with gender politics, and Paul used a lot of rhetorical energy to establish his authority in that assembly. Whether his appeals were successful we do not know.

Richard Horsley acknowledges that, while Paul proclaimed an alternative gospel and an alternative emperor, and built an alternative assembly in the city of Corinth, he "reinscribed" imperial images and relations within his arguments aimed at reinforcing the discipline of an anti-imperial movement. Such imperial language could only reinforce relations of subordination within the assembly.[43]

The later letters written in Paul's name picked up on these texts suggesting submission and obedience to male authority and ran with it.[44] The deutero-Pauline letters Colossians and Ephesians introduce the complete form of the household code that orders relationships between wife and husband, slave and master, and father and son.[45] The central interest of these texts lies in reinforcing the submission and obedience of the socially weaker group—wives, slaves, and children—and in confirming the authority of the head of the household, the *paterfamilias*.[46] Although the code appears in its fullest form in later letters, the injunction to submissiveness does nevertheless appear in the authentic Pauline writings of Romans 13 and 1 Corinthians 11. It provides the rationale for self-regulating submission to authority and, from the other side, gentle rulership. "Wives, be subject to your husbands, as is fitting in the Lord. Husbands, love your wives and never treat them harshly. . . . Slaves, obey your earthly masters . . . fearing in the Lord. Masters, treat your slaves justly and fairly, for you know that you have a Master in heaven" (Colossians 3:18—4:1). These behaviors are exemplary of what it means to clothe yourselves with love and let the peace of Christ rule in your hearts (Colossians 3:14-15; compare Ephesians 5:22—6:9). This has been called "love patriarchalism," a phrase signifying Christian appropriation of the patriarchal household codes.[47] Love patriarchalism is a very useful label for "hierarchical relationships of male dominance and female, child, and slave subordination . . . accepted and maintained as normative, but with the understanding there was now an inner equality in Christ."[48] Such patriarchalism is not representative of Jesus' views, and some would say it does not represent the authentic Paul either. But it served a significant (which is not to say legitimate) political purpose: it provided the ideology of obedience/authority in the household, consisting of a wife, children, and one or more slaves, and it functioned as the model of the state. If the family was not ruled faithfully, the state was believed to be jeopardized.[49]

Love patriarchalism is incompatible with the ethos of democracy and equality, marks of a genuine challenge to Roman hierarchical political and social forms. Yet it is precisely an ethos of democracy and equality that will be necessary to undergird any efforts to curtail greenhouse gas emissions, for such efforts will require broad-based support and consistent practice for the long term to be effective.

Paul Had Little Concern to Effect System Change in the City-States Where the "Israelites" Were Living

Paul's missionary efforts to the so-called Gentiles were directed to Israelite minorities living among non-Israelite majority populations. The Israelites were resident aliens or perhaps citizens.[50] This view, informed by cultural anthropology, of who the "Gentiles" were, undercuts the received view of Paul's universalism, the view that he took the Israelite tradition and extended the notion of who could be included in the covenant with Israel's God to the many peoples who did not share the identity of the Judeans.

When Paul, a Pharisaic Israelite, writes that he was sent to "the Gentiles" (in English translations), it would better be translated as "the other peoples." This formulation better captures the cultural assumption of first-century Palestine regarding the significance of the "Ingroup," and the insignificance of the "Outgroup": the Israelites (Judeans, otherwise translated "Jews") are the focus of Paul's concerns, as this group is constitutive of his own identity. The Judeans are the Ingroup of which he is part. Coming from a high-context culture, Paul would not have thought it necessary to explain that to his readers. Paul went to Israelites who lived among other peoples of the Mediterranean, Israelites located in Greco-Roman cities. That is what he meant when he called himself "apostle to the Gentiles."

At least one exception to this generalization is evident in the Letter to the Romans (chapters 9–11), as Paul addresses the question of why all the Israelites did not believe that their God had raised Jesus from the dead. In the course of this discussion, he addresses Israelite Jesus group members and also and separately a number of non-Israelites who had joined the Jesus group. Because he deals with the question of non-Israelites separately, it would appear that the presence of such non-Israelites in the Jesus group was exceptional.[51] Paul deals with the fact that some non-Israelites adopted faith in the God of Israel and in God's raising Israel's Messiah Jesus from the dead, while some of the Israelites did not. Paul understands God's purpose to be to provoke among law-observant Israelites a concern for what is rightfully their own (Romans 11:11). God has allowed non-Israelites to adopt this faith to "make Israel jealous."

But Paul seems to lack enthusiasm for the non-Israelites; in Romans 11:17-24 he compared Israel to a cultivated olive tree, and non-Israelites to wild olive shoots grafted on. He contrasts the "natural" branches (according to nature) of the Israelites to the grafts "contrary to nature" of the non-Israelites. The language of "contrary to nature" is what he employed in Romans 1 referring to the sexual behavior of the Romans.[52] His Mediterranean audience would know that the branches of the wild olive would not bear fruit. Paul's ethnocentrism is on display in this discussion.[53]

In most other instances, Paul addresses his letters to Israelites who are resident among other peoples, alerting them that the kingdom of heaven, "an Israelite theocracy," was coming. It would be ushered in by Jesus as Israel's Messiah in the Davidic line. Paul knew that the kingdom of heaven was imminent because after the Romans executed Jesus, God raised him from the dead. The "theocracy" was to be based in Palestine, with Jerusalem as the capital. This "good news" was good news for Israelites, as it came through a revelation from Israel's God, about Israel's Messiah and an Israelite theocracy, according to Israel's Scriptures.[54]

At times in his letters, Paul refers to his mission among the "uncircumcised." According to the post–sixth-century talmudic idea of "Jewishness,"[55] contemporary readers may assume that this term refers to what in today's language would be termed "non-Jews." However, this assumption is probably not accurate. Male infant cutting as a distinguishing Judean marker can be dated to 150 B.C.E. and the Maccabean reforms, and probably several centuries later among Yahweh worshipers far from the region of Judea.[56] In the Diaspora, circumcision entailed cutting a nick in the foreskin, not the removal of the foreskin as in the practice of circumcision today. "Josephus reports a number of Israelites had their foreskins resewn so they might appear whole when present in the baths of the period. . . . In order to prevent such concealment of Israelite affiliation, in 150 C.E. Pharisaic scribes determined the whole foreskin must be removed to fulfill the requirement of the law."[57] It is not inconsistent, then, for Paul to see himself as the apostle to the uncircumcised, meaning the Israelites living away from Judea in Greco-Roman cities. "Many Israelites resident among non-Israelites were far along the way of assimilation, including adopting local worship patterns."[58]

Thus, in the parts of Paul's letters that refer to what translations render "Jews and Greeks," it would be more accurate to translate "Judean and Hellenist," which carried the valence of "barbarian Israelites and civilized Israelites."[59]

The focal proclamation undergirding Paul's efforts among the civilized Israelites concerns the coming of the Messiah, "the day of the Lord." In Israel's Scriptures this day would mark God's restoration and salvation of *Israel*.[60]

The use of cultural anthropology as a lens through which to read the letters of Paul presents some very new perspectives about which serious critical review will need a few more years to do its work. However, the most controversial component of this way of reading the letters of Paul concerns his mission, his "target population." For our purposes, we do not need to wait for that consensus to form, for some conclusions would have a general bearing on the ethics of climate change policies regardless of whether Paul defined his mission as being to Israelites in non-Israelite lands. We are able to see these things through the lenses that bring into focus Paul's response to the Roman hierarchy and his tendency to reproduce an alternative hierarchy in which he reserves for himself a key place in mediating the people's access to Christ's Holy Spirit, the Winds of God:

- Paul challenged the ideology of the cult of the emperor. By definition, he was political.

- He replaced the emperor god with the Lord of Israel.
- He anticipated the coming apocalypse as the occasion for Jesus Messiah to redeem the children of Israel along with all the rest of God's creation, including plants, animals, and all of the cosmos. Creation has fundamental significance.
- He launched his mission to alert Israelites, minority populations (whom he called "Gentiles") living in the Greco-Roman cities among other peoples, or a more general target population named as "Gentiles," that God was about to do a great thing—restore Israel to its former greatness, with Jesus as the Messiah leading the challenge to the Roman Empire. The collection for the saints in Jerusalem was a sign consistent with the prophets of Israel that people from all the nations were streaming to God's holy mount, bringing gifts and praising the God of Israel.
- Paul saw no point in addressing social systems. If he welcomed into the *ekklēsia*, as some of the early gatherings did, women and slaves independently of the "father of the household," he did not propose alternative structures of family or strategize about how to overturn the slave system. Nor did he propose that the *ekklēsia* see as its mission to offer a challenge to the Roman Empire about how to organize society.

The common ground of the biblical scholarship that I have surveyed holds Paul to be a challenge to the civil religion of empire as false, as idolatry. Insofar as his mission was propelled by the Isaian idea of the restoration of the Davidic kinship of the children of Israel, of all the peoples of the world, and of the whole of creation, his plumb line was the jubilee justice of God. Insofar as he was focused on convincing his fellow "Israelites" that Jesus was the crucified and risen Messiah, the justice of God may have been secondary. It is difficult to draw inferences about the relevance of Paul's project to ours until this matter is further clarified.

PART THREE

Biblical Social Ethics
and the Kingdom of Oil

CHAPTER EIGHT

The Atmospheric Global Commons

Bless the Lord, O my soul!
O Lord my God, you are very great.
You are clothed with honor and majesty,
wrapped in light as with a garment.
You stretched out the heavens like a tent,
you set the beams of your chambers on the waters,
you make the clouds your chariot,
    you ride on the wings of the wind,
you make the winds your messengers,
    fire and flame your ministers.

You set the earth on its foundations,
    so that it shall never be shaken.
You cover it with the deep as with a garment;
    the waters stood above the mountains.
At your rebuke they flee;
    at the sound of your thunder they take to flight.

They rose up to the mountains,
    ran down to the valleys,
    to the place that you appointed for them.
You set a boundary that they may not pass,
    so that they might not again cover the earth.

You make springs gush forth in the valleys;
    they flow between the hills,
giving drink to every wild animal;
    The wild asses quench their thirst.
By the streams the birds of the air have their habitation;
    they sing among the branches.
From your lofty abode you water the mountains;
    The earth is satisfied with the fruit of your work.

You cause the grass to grow for the cattle,
    and plants for people to cultivate,
    to bring forth food from the earth,
    and wine to gladden the human heart,
oil to make our faces shine,
    And bread to strengthen the human heart.
The trees of the Lord are watered abundantly,
    The cedars of Lebanon that God planted.
In them the birds build their nests;
    the stork has her home in the fir trees.
The high mountains are for the wild goats;
    The rocks are a refuge for the badgers.
You have made the moon to mark the seasons;
    the sun knows its time for setting.
You make darkness, and it is night,
    when all the animals of the forest come creeping out.
The young lions roar for their prey,
    seeking their food from God.
When the sun rises, they withdraw and lie down in their
    dens.
People go out to their work and to their labor until the
    evening.

O Lord, how manifold are your works!
In wisdom you have made them all;
 The earth is full of your creatures.
Yonder is the sea, great and wide, creeping things innu-
  merable are there,
 living things both small and great.
There go the ships,
 and Leviathan that you formed to sport in it.

These all look to you
 to give them their food in due season;
When you give to them, they gather it up;
 when you open your hand, they are filled with good
  things.
When you hide your face, they are dismayed;
 when you take away their breath, they die
 and return to their dust.
When you send forth your spirit, they are created;
 And you renew the face of the ground.

May the glory of the Lord endure forever,
 may the Lord rejoice in her works,
who looks on the earth and it trembles,
 who touches the mountains and they smoke!
I will sing to the Lord as long as I live;
 I will sing praise to my God while I have being.
May my meditation be pleasing to God, for I rejoice in
 the Lord.
Let sinners be consumed from the earth, and let the
 wicked be no more!
Bless the Lord, O my soul!
Praise the Lord! (Psalm 104)

The Psalms, including Psalm 104, were used in the temple
liturgy, sung by the priests. We have no direct evidence that
Jesus of Nazareth knew or cited the Psalms, though in Luke's
Gospel he is depicted as referring to the Torah, the Prophets,

and the Writings (which include the Psalms).[1] Tradition in Mark recalls Jesus citing from Psalms 22, 110, and perhaps 62, but not Psalm 104.

Psalm 104 is a beautiful psalm, extolling the marvel of creation independent of its value to humankind. This poem is probably an adaptation of an Egyptian hymn from about 1365 B.C.E., a pre-Israelite hymn.[2] It therefore represents a universalistic thread in Hebrew Scriptures, a thread that exists alongside the more nationalistic threads. Our use of Psalm 104 is consistent with our purpose of reading and interpreting the Scriptures in a way that serves the common good, the good of all the nations and their ecosystems.

This Psalm makes reference to many of the major life-support systems: the wind currents in the air envelope; salt-water oceans, freshwater streams, and the hydrologic cycle; forests, grasslands, and croplands; mountain ranges; and the solar and lunar cycles. The psalm celebrates habitat for all the creatures and agriculture for humankind.

The wind in this poem exercises its own agency, carrying God's messages.

The ancients perceived the winds as having their effect in unknown and unknowable ways; the winds blow where and when they will and can produce unbelievably overwhelming effects. The ancients associated the wind with the activity of God. Holy Spirit, or God's Spirit, also refers to God's activity.[3]

In this psalm, God's messengers are in and from the sky, bringing the message to the land. The sky/land is a part of our whole life, life today as opposed to the next life. The messengers are not necessarily angels but nevertheless indicate God's presence among us.[4] The wind as God's presence among us brings us the evidence of pervasive practices of pollution, and the buildup of climate-forcing gases. The unusual power of the wind today is generated by the heating of the climate system. It is evidence of the energy created by the heating of the oceans, when the warmer water is not able to absorb the amount of CO_2 climatologists had calculated. So CO_2 in the

air is growing faster than it did per year in 1990–99 (3.3 percent per year now, compared to 1.3 percent earlier.)[5] In turn,
the oceans will heat faster and the power of the wind will
increase.

The Reign of God Requires Healthy Communities
in Healthy Ecosystems

Jesus taught his listeners that they had the capacity for historical agency, and a component of that capacity was the power
to engage the Scriptures and the priestly authorities directly,
or to disengage strategically. They had their own authority in
moral reflection. We too will call up the traditions that nurture
us in wisdom and support community solidarity, responsibility,
and truth telling. The Scriptures, critically read, can reveal and
encourage such wisdom, solidarity, responsibility, and truth
telling. But without the active agency of the people in interpreting and choosing how to foreground stories and commandments, the Scriptures can also be the tools of our pacification,
domination, or alienation.

The perspective on Jesus' ministry that I have developed in this book uses biblical scholarship that depicts Jesus
encouraging local communities to withdraw from the imperial structure and establish parallel economies. Jesus the Galilean was rooted in a different geography than Judea where
the temple was, and where temple politics focused. He participated in the temple rituals, but he also offered healing
and God's forgiveness in the village setting, the effect of
which was to challenge the centralization of rites and discharge of debt obligation in Jerusalem. As one consequence,
the capacity of the temple to collect tithes was weakened.
For people on the land facing heavy debt pressures, the effect
of Jesus' invitation to local healing and local forgiveness was
debt relief. In this light, the import of Jesus' ministry was to
call attention to the debt relief code in the Mosaic covenant.
Using several parables, he pointed the poor to the reign of
God in earthy terms:

the land or resources necessary for common livelihood and independence belonged to them;

the efforts of the people on the soil would be rewarded generously, with a harvest they could eat;

nature's processes are mysterious, and we can cooperate with them to ensure a plentiful harvest;

toil, persistent toil for someone else is wrong. The reign of God means living with the fruit of the land without the toil for someone else;

the reign of God and its plenty is not only for humankind; it is also for wild kind, on this earth.

Using oblique parables, masking the challenge they represented to the temple priests and the Roman governor, Jesus healed, opened the possibility of forgiveness, and ate and drank with others, nourishing the social capital necessary to sustain the people in small communities, bearing up under foreign domination but embedded in their ecologies.

One implication: the measure of an *economy* is its capacity to ensure the health of the people in the community, the community constituted by the complexity and diversity of plant and animal neighborhoods. Generation of wealth is not the first measure of a good economy because wealth, when it exists alongside poverty, is suspect.

Another implication: Likewise, governance and religious practices should be internal to communities, accountable to moral standards generated by foundational experiences of community development. By community development is meant the growth in the health of persons and the rest of nature within their respective habitats.[6] These standards should be testable by all, not limited to an elite whose status verges on the sacred.

The kingdom of God, the inheritance from God, is not an ideal or an "impossible possibility" but an alternative to the imperial powers that appropriate the earth for the benefit of the Kingdom of Oil. Today the inheritance from God is an alternative to the Kingdom of Oil, requiring just solutions to the suffering of the planet, perpetrated by the "oil boys." Wisdom is required for discerning the outlines of this inheritance.

Rather than a big cataclysmic event in the future that ends history as we know it, the inheritance from God will have to be discovered in the process of step by step learning how to step aside from the petroleum economy and become citizens of the world house.

An Alternative to the Kingdom of Oil

The flexibility mechanisms embedded in the Kyoto Protocol (International Emission Trading, Joint Implementation, and the Clean Development Mechanism) are based on the effort to establish a market in air where there has been none. It is preferable to discourage cement manufacturers and energy corporations from dumping into the air as if there were no consequences to them. However, establishing a market in atmosphere will not suffice. Additional policies represent direct challenges to the Kingdom of Oil.

Address All Forms of Subsidies That Are Currently Benefiting Fossil Fuel Use

Both consumer and producer subsidies are forestalling the transition to solar and wind energy. In the case of the so-called developing countries, to establish infrastructure that mimics the fossil-fuel–based infrastructure of northern Europe and North America locks in or predetermines too much future production and transportation on the carbon path. If subsidies for petroleum/natural gas/coal energy are withdrawn in the industrialized nations, the incentive for alternative research and development will increase.

> Energy subsidies make automation, petrochemical fertilizers, and long-distance transportation seem cheaper, thus giving an added boost to large-scale, industrial-style agriculture. They also improve the economics of fishing, mining, chemical production, virgin paper manufacture, and virgin minerals processing.[7]

Because fossil fuels require highly centralized capitalization for their development, they involve support for strong-arm politics to guarantee their delivery systems, which militate against the possibility for community autonomy, or what Roman Catholic social teachings calls the principle of subsidiarity. Withdrawing subsidies for big oil is necessary to move on to other political possibilities that are more reflective of the communities of commensality that Jesus seemed to be supporting.

Besides "getting the prices right," which subsidies thwart and emissions credits attempt to approach, other policies to lower greenhouse gas emissions include boosting efficiency standards, forging industry covenants, supporting new energy supplies, and storing carbon, primarily by protecting tropical, temperate, and boreal forests.[8]

Support Renewable Energy Projects That Require Local Employment and a Local Skill Base

The wind is a messenger about the effects of climate change toward global warming. In addition, wind promises to be a path out of the Kingdom of Oil. Since it is fossil fuels that are generating most of the GHGs, finding ways to substitute wind, solar, and geothermal energy for energy from coal and oil is a major strategy for healing the earth.

The scientists of the Intergovernmental Panel on Climate Change (IPCC) are among many policy theorists who believe that renewable sources of energy allow for smaller and more distributed power plants appropriate to the conditions of different geographies, and making way for local communities to enjoy their inheritance from God. This is the promise: that renewable energy will result in local employment, a local skill base, less vulnerability to sabotage or to the grid system failures that affect large sections of the country.

The promise of renewable energy may not be fulfilled, however, unless political processes ensure it. The mixed blessing of wind energy can be illustrated by a wind farm developed in 2001 in Gray County in western Kansas, where the economy has historically depended on agriculture. Kansas ranks third among the states in wind power potential, behind North Dakota and Texas. In the Kansas Farm Bureau publication highlighting the wind farm, the largest in Kansas, the benefits of siting the wind farm are described. The county has about six thousand residents and Montezuma, the small town closest to the 170 windmills, or wind turbines, has a population of 995. The energy corporation that developed the wind farm is generating enough electricity to power thirty-three thousand homes. The power that it generates goes to a utility company for people in Missouri, not to the people who live in the immediate area.

What is the wind energy corporation that is investing in western Kansas? It is Florida Power and Light (FPL), based in Juno Beach, Florida, a company that has power-generation assets in more than twenty states. It is also the majority owner and operator of nuclear power plants. The energy corporation makes a significant annual donation to the county of about $330,000. The county then distributes funds to the public school system (about $152,000); to the township, which supports the hospital, library, and cemetery; to the county rural fire district; and to the county itself. The county puts their portion into the general fund to reduce the mill levy for residents.[9]

This arrangement has favorable aspects but at the same time generates some serious questions. The donation from the corporation has a sizable impact on the local economy and the capacity of the local government to provide services for the citizens. But what will happen if the corporation decides to disinvest? The negotiated agreement is for ten years, renewable for another ten years. What then? Will this rural county take a $330,000 hit in public funds? The community does not really control the energy that the wind blowing in their ecology produces.

In addition, the persistent downside to wind energy production has been bird kills. The birds cannot see the blades of the turbine when they are spinning fast, and they fly into their death trap. The people of the San Francisco Bay area have been alerted to this problem because of proximity to the Altamont Pass, where approximately five thousand wind turbines have been generating electricity since the early 1980s. Coastal cool air is sucked inland by the heat of the San Joaquin Valley, creating strong winds whose path is the pass. A 2004 California Energy Commission report estimated that total bird kills at the installation are between 1,766 and 4,221 annually, including fatalities of golden eagles, red-tailed hawks, American kestrals, and burrowing owls.

A legal settlement involving wildlife groups, wind companies, and Alameda County regulators was forged to reduce the deaths of these raptors by half. The settlement called for the shutdown or relocation of three hundred of the most lethal turbines, which are older, smaller, and shorter and generate in the one hundred kilowatt range. They are to be replaced with newer, more powerful (generating to three megawatts) and taller turbines whose blades turn more slowly. The higher blades will avoid the raptors that dive for their prey, and, with the more powerful turbines, fewer of them will be necessary.

Sadly, the problem is not simply birds running into the blades. Many dead birds have been found around turbines that were turned off. Some have been electrocuted; some apparently killed by predators.

The number of the turbines at Altamont, plus their location on a bird migratory route, are key factors in their lethal effect. The Scientific Review Committee monitoring bird deaths has lengthened the list of turbines to be removed or relocated, and has asked that, in addition to shutting down the turbines in November and December, the shutdown be extended through February. It would cost one billion dollars to fully replace the older with the newer turbines.[10]

Bats are also attracted to wind turbines, a fatal attraction, but only half the bat corpses found near turbine bases near Alberta,

Canada, showed physical evidence of being hit by a blade. Ninety percent showed signs of internal hemorrhaging. The hypothesis is that a small zone of low pressure about a yard in diameter is created at the tips of the blades. When bats fly through this area, their lungs expand, and the fine capillaries around the edges of the lungs burst. This ailment is called "barotrauma" and is a condition related to the bends that affects divers.[11]

Bats are at particular risk during migration periods in late summer and early fall. The majority of the bats killed by wind turbines are species that rely on trees as roosts throughout the year and migrate long distances. When this phenomenon was reported in August 2008, it was thought the placement of the turbines is the cause of the bat deaths, and that some turbine sites are not in the migration paths of bats. But the Fort Collins Science Center reported in 2009 that bat fatalities have now been documented at nearly every wind facility in North America where adequate surveys for bats have been conducted, and several of these sites are estimated to cause the deaths of thousands of bats per year.[12] The mystery of why bats die at turbine sites remains unsolved, but it matters.

A spokesperson from one of the firms that owns turbines at the pass said that "the impact on birds has to be weighed against the human deaths and diseases that are reduced by using wind power instead of pollution-producing fossil fuels." Is that a justifiable response? It would qualify as a descriptor of the A1 future, where the whole world becomes a garden cultivated for human purposes. It is my hope that people rooted in Hebrew Scriptures and the New Testament will be sickened and saddened contemplating such a future, and for this reason will press wind companies to adopt bird-protective measures.

The birds and bats ride on the wings of the wind and have their habitation by the springs in the valleys. They matter to the singer of the psalm. Already the earth is experiencing a decrease in bird and bat populations. We have to listen to the messenger wind to know whether it is possible to power our homes, schools, offices, and shops without destroying the original creatures who ride on the wings of the wind.

By the way, FPL Energy is the company with the most turbines in the Altamont Pass. FPL is also co-owner of SEGS solar power plants, the largest array in the world, located in the Mojave Desert. FPL is an energy corporation. It is developing renewable power to meet the growing demand of utility companies that are mandated to include a certain percentage of renewable power in the total package supporting the utility. Their main accountability structure, however, is their stockholders. Rural western Kansas is a place where wind is very strong, but the corporation has no long-term commitment to the health of the particular people, plants, and animals who live there. It is not indigenous to that place. It is making a contribution to the effort to decrease greenhouse gases, but is it showing us a path out of the Kingdom of Oil? Or is it dressing up the old power in new duds?

An interesting dimension of this story is the fact that the article describing the wind farm in Gray County in western Kansas, and provoking me to visit, is in a rural-targeted magazine.[13] The author depicts a favorable relationship between the people of this county and the wind energy producer. Farmers and ranchers who have wind turbines sited on their land have the option of choosing a royalty payment based on a percentage of the production from the turbines located on their ground, or they may elect to receive a flat fee. The farmers and ranchers are discovering that they have royalty rights to wind that blows over their land. Wind power, and therefore renewable power, companies are building coalitions with farmers and ranchers, who for various reasons—not the least of which is the low gas mileage their pickup trucks average—have blocked the serious consideration of a carbon tax. Now they have an incentive to increase the amount of wind energy that goes into electricity.

The question of scale is relevant to geothermal energy also. Geothermal energy has proven technology and abundant resources, but only a small fraction of geothermal potential has been developed so far. Not all geothermal technologies are sustainable. When hot water from the earth is brought to the surface to generate electricity or to heat directly, it is then injected back into a well, storage pond, or river. In this case, either the ground-heated water or its temperature is depleted over time. Recovery is likely, but only when the resource is taken out of production. During production, some environmental consequences are risked: changes to the landscape, emissions into surface and subsurface waters, noise, land subsidence and earthquakes, plus solid waste.[14] However, smaller scale geothermal heat pumps using a closed loop and heat transfer system to heat and cool homes and other buildings do not require high earth temperatures, and can generate energy for both heating and cooling just about anywhere. Because no liquid is extracted from the earth nor returned to the earth, this technology is sustainable and is appropriate for individual residences, educational and commercial buildings.[15]

Geothermal energy is already being used around the globe to heat buildings, grow plants in greenhouses, dehydrate onions and garlic, dry grains and woods, heat water for fish farming and for raising alligators, pasteurize milk, warm roads and sidewalks to melt snow, and for balneology or spas. Small countries, like Iceland, Norway, Israel, Switzerland, Denmark, and Georgia are using geothermal energy at the highest rate given their land mass and population. The countries with the largest installed capacity are the United States, Sweden, China, Iceland, and Turkey.[16] This renewable energy will be developed more and more, but not all applications are sustainable, even if they do result in fewer greenhouse gas emissions.

The promise of renewable energy sources has been that they will lower our production of global warming gases and provide the capacity for local and regional communities to power themselves and sustain their local/regional economies. What concerns me is energy policy oriented toward or used mainly by large energy corporations investing in renewable power for their shareholders. The use of renewable energy is preferable to oil, coal, and natural gas (the latter has been described as a transition fuel), but the political vision of the biblical texts is of sustainable communities. We will have to step up political efforts if we share this hope with the biblical texts.

Community Wind, Community Sun, Community of the Soil, Enlivened Communities

And it is possible to do so. Already some nations in Europe and some states in this country have enacted policies supporting "community wind" over corporate wind. "Corporate wind" refers to large-scale projects such as that in Gray County, Kansas, and the Altamont Pass, projects that are often fifty megawatts (MW) in capacity or larger. They are the centerpiece of the B1 vision of the future. "Community wind" structures vary depending on ownership, but they are locally owned and operated, small-scale projects, twenty megawatts or less. The path to community wind is to corporate wind what the path to solar panels on every rooftop is to solar arrays covering acres in the Mojave Desert. I submit to you that community wind and solar panels on every rooftop are the centerpiece of the B2 vision of the future.

By 2000, community-owned wind power constituted 88 percent (5400 MW) of German and 84 percent (1900 MW) of Danish wind power. The Germans and Danes together accounted for just under 50 percent of the world's installed wind-power capacity at that time.[17]

In the United States, policy has focused on corporate wind. But we have successful examples of community wind, particularly in Minnesota and Iowa, where rural landowners and local communities engaged in policy making. "In 2005 Minnesota enacted its Community-Based Energy Development (C-BED) legislation, which requires all the state's electric utilities to offer front-end–loaded advanced renewable energy tariffs for locally owned wind projects."[18]

The development of community wind in Iowa took a different course, stimulated by schools that took advantage of state financing and net metering to develop projects with one or two commercial-scale wind turbines. Rural landowners and local community groups then became involved in projects, and the state legislature passed a production tax credit of 1.5 cents per kilowatt hour and sold renewable energy certificates

(REGs), which together have increased the attractiveness of community wind.[19]

Policies such as those that Minnesota and Iowa have developed have proven to be cost-effective in that they create markets in which community wind competes successfully with large developers. If community wind is desired, however, then the policies should be monitored to determine whether corporate wind is in fact taking more advantage.

Why would nations or states take steps to nurture community wind? These projects provide clean, renewable electricity without contributing to global warming. But they also stimulate local economies more than corporate wind, increase local energy independence, increase competition in energy markets, delay the need for new transmission lines, and help diversify local economies and create new income sources for farmers, landowners, and communities.[20] Of the 11,603 MW of wind installed in the United States, 421 MW are community owned. Such projects are currently operating in at least twenty states. But the growth in community wind has been slow, owing to such barriers as the inability of individual investors to use tax credits efficiently, to select a viable ownership structure to match their needs, to finance projects and reap economies of scale, to escape contractual constraints that limit on-site opportunities, and to connect to the distribution grid.[21] Yet the midwestern states have long histories with grain cooperatives, and those cultures and histories can help to minimize these barriers and stimulate community effort to fly with the wind.

Treaties with mechanisms to incentivize energy, cement, and automobile corporations to lower their emissions and to transition to a noncarbon base deserve our support. But it would be wrong to wait for treaty negotiators and highly capitalized interests to heal the harm done to earth's air envelope. At the local and regional level is great potential to bypass those laggard interests, to step aside from their paths, and instead to soar with the wind, soak up the sun, be rooted in the soil, and enspirit our communities.

NOTES

Introduction

1. www.coolcalifornia.org. Depending on where you live, you may have access to a carbon calculator. In your search engine, enter your city or region + carbon calculator.

Chapter One

1. Carbon released from burning fossil fuel and making cement rose from 1.3 percent per year in 1990–99 to 3.3 percent per year in 2000–2006, a much faster rate of growth than anticipated. Causal factors include increased use of fossil fuels coupled with a decline in the gas absorbed by the warming oceans. In terms of tonnage, whereas the burning of fossil fuel and making of cement sent 7.0 billion metric tons per year in 2000, by 2006 it was 8.4 billion metric tons. A metric ton is 2,205 pounds. See Randolph E. Schmid, "CO_2 in Air Growing Faster Than Expected," *San Francisco Chronicle*, October 23, 2007, A13; and idem, "Greenhouse Gases Growing Faster Than Ever, Report Says," *San Francisco Chronicle*, April 24, 2008, A9.

2. Executive Office of the President of the United States, Office of Science and Technology Policy, *Climate Change: State of Knowledge* (Washington, D.C., October 1997), 9. The observed CO_2 concentration in 2005 was about 380 ppm, according to the "Technical Summary: A

Report accepted by Working Group II of the Intergovernmental Panel on Climate Change but not approved in detail. Available at http://www .ipcc.ch/.

3. H. Josef Hebert, "New Proof of Severe Global Warming," *San Francisco Chronicle*, October 26, 2000, A3.

4. For a description of the roles and interests of these nations, including more on developing nations, China, India, and Japan, see Sebastian Oberthür and Hermann E. Ott, *The Kyoto Protocol: International Climate Policy for the 21st Century* (Berlin/New York: Springer, 1999), 13–32.

5. See Office of Science and Technology Policy, *Climate Change: State of Knowledge*, 12–15.

6. A text of the Kyoto Protocol and background material on it can be found at http://unfccc.int/Kyoto_protocol. The background material makes the point that the Protocol shares the objectives and institutions of the United Nations Framework Convention on Climate Change. The major distinction between the two is that, while the Convention *encouraged* developed countries to stabilize GHG emissions, the Protocol *commits* them to do so. The Kyoto Protocol is, then, the first addition to the UNFCCC treaty.

7. T. Barker, I. Bashmakov, L. Bernstein, et al., "Technical Summary," in *Climate Change 2007: Mitigation of Climate Change. Contribution of Working Group III to the Fourth Assessment Report of the Intergovernmental Panel on Climate Change* (Cambridge/New York: Cambridge University Press, 2007), 31.

8. "[I]ncreases in global mean temperature would produce net economic losses in many developing countries for all magnitudes of warming studied . . . and losses would be greater in magnitude the higher the level of warming. . . . In contrast, an increase in global mean temperature of up to a few degrees C would produce a mixture of economic gains and losses in developed countries . . . , with economic losses for larger temperature increases. . . . The projected distribution of economic impacts is such that it would increase the disparity in well-being between developed countries and developing countries, with disparity growing for higher projected temperature increases. . . . The more damaging impacts estimated for developing countries reflects, in part, their lesser adaptive capacity relative to developed countries." From *Climate Change 2001: Impacts, Adaptation, and Vulnerability; Contribution of Working Group II to the Third Assessment Report of the Intergovernmental Panel on Climate Change* (approved in detail at the Sixth Session of IPCC Working Group II, Geneva, Switzerland, February 13–16, 2001) (Cambridge/New York: Cambridge University Press, 2001), "Summary for Policymakers," par. 2.8.

9. With the exception that within the industrialized nations are indigenous communities in which traditional lifestyles are followed, and who have little capacity and few options for adaptation. See IPCC, *Climate Change 2001: Impacts, Adaptation, and Vulnerability*, Summary for Policymakers, 16.

10. The Intergovernmental Panel on Climate Change (IPCC) was established in 1988 by the United Nations Environment Programme (UNEP) and the World Meteorological Organization (WMO). All states that are members of the United Nations and of the WMO are therefore members of the IPCC and its three working groups. Working Group 1 on the science of climate change, Working Group 2 on scientific-technical analyses of impacts and mitigation of climate change, and Working Group 3 on the economic and social dimensions of climate change. Because of the range of study topics, the IPCC is a hybrid body, partly political and partly scientific and technical. The working groups prepare summaries for policy-makers for each of their studies. The summaries are drafted and reviewed by hundreds of experts from all over the world. These experts are nominated by governments as well as by non-governmental organizations (NGOs), but they are to act in their personal capacities. The summaries are read carefully and approved by representatives of the member states, though the full reports are "accepted" without discussion. In this light, the work of the IPCC can be seen to be filtered before dissemination, which makes their findings even more remarkable.

11. Barker et al., "Technical Summary," in *Climate Change 2007: Mitigation*, 31.

12. Sonja Boehmer-Christiansen and Aynsley Kellow, *International Environmental Policy: Interests and Failure of the Kyoto Process* (Cheltenham, UK/Northampton, Mass.: Edward Elgar, 2002), 54.

13. Article 2 of the Convention, as cited in Oberthür and Ott, *Kyoto Protocol*, 33. This source provides a thorough account of the climate policies that preceded and emerged from the Kyoto conference. Much of this introduction to the Protocol relies on this text.

14. Sir Nicholas Stern, *The Stern Review: The Economics of Climate Change* (http://www.hm-treasury.gov.uk/IndependentReviews/Sternreview economicsclimatechange/stern reviewindex.cfm).

15. Andrew E. Dessler and Edward A. Parson, *The Science and Politics of Global Climate Change; A Guide to the Debate* (Cambridge/New York: Cambridge University Press, 2006), 44.

16. Ibid., 148.

17. http://www.ipcc.ch/

18. The Montreal Protocol (1987) regulates ozone-depleting halocarbons, and those the Kyoto process does not regulate. Non–ozone-depleting

halocarbons, such as hydrofluorocarbons, perfluorocarbons (PFCs), and sulphur hexafluoride (SF_6) are regulated by Kyoto.

19. According to Oberthür and Ott (*Kyoto Protocol*, 9), in developing countries the sources of GHGs are somewhat different, though fossil fuel combustion still accounts for the largest quantity of GHGs, because tropical deforestation accounted for between 15 and 25 percent of global CO_2 emissions in the early 1990s. Methane is a higher percentage because of rice paddies in Asia.

20. UNFCCC Secretariat and IEA, 1997, cited in Oberthür and Ott, *Kyoto Protocol*, 22. The sources of CO_2 in the year 2000 are as follows: world emissions from burning fossil fuels (coal, oil, and natural gas), which provide 80 percent of global human energy use resulted in 6.4 billion metric tons of carbon (GtC); from net deforestation worldwide, but principally in the tropics, 1.6 GtC; from chemical processes involved in manufacturing cement, 0.2 GtC. These factors bring the total emissions of CO_2 in the year 2000 to about 8 GtC. Depending on which directions the world's nations take in the future, the year 2100 could witness as little as 5 GtC or as much as 30 GtC generated per year. See Dessler and Parson, *Science and Politics of Global Climate Change*, 78, 96.

21. The targeted reductions accepted at Kyoto range from 8 percent (EU countries plus many Eastern European parties); 7 percent for the United States; 6 percent for Canada, Hungary, Japan, and Poland; 5 percent for Croatia. New Zealand, the Russian Federation, and Ukraine agreed to stabilize at 1990 levels. However, Norway got concessions to increase by 1 percent, Australia by 8 percent, and Iceland by 10 percent. See Oberthür and Ott, *Kyoto Protocol*, 129.

22. Organization for Economic Co-operation and Development, International Energy Agency, *International Emission Trading: From Concept to Reality* (Paris: Organization for Economic Cooperation and Development, International Energy Agency, 2001), 19.

23. Ibid., 47.

24. Herman Verhagen and Jaap van der Sar, "United Air Fund: Towards a Just Distribution of the Consumption of the Atmosphere," paper to the World Council of Churches Consultation on "Equity and Emission Trading: Ethical and Theological Dimensions," Saskatoon, Canada, May 2000, 3.

25. Organization for Economic Co-operation and Development, International Energy Agency, *International Emission Trading*, 22.

26. Warwick J. McKibben and Peter J. Wilcoxen, *Climate Change Policy after Kyoto: A Blueprint for a Realistic Approach* (Washington, D.C.: Brookings Institution Press, 2002), 49.

27. Organization for Economic Co-operation and Development, International Energy Agency, *International Emission Trading*, 25.

28. Boehmer-Christiansen and Kellow, *International Environmental Policy*, 65.

29. Christian Egenhofer, "The Compatibility of the Kyoto Mechanisms with Traditional Environmental Instruments," in Carlo Carraro and Christian Egenhofer, *Firms, Governments and Climate Policy: Incentive-based Policies for Long-term Climate Change* (Cheltenham, UK/Northampton, Mass.: Edward Elgar, 2003), 31.

30. McKibbin and Wilcoxen, *Climate Change Policy after Kyoto*, 46.

31. Boehmer-Christiansen and Kellow, *International Environmental Policy*, 67.

32. Jiro Akita, "A Simple Model of CDM Low-Hanging Fruit," in *International Frameworks and Technological Strategies to Prevent Climate Change*, ed. Takamitsu Sawa (Tokyo/New York: Springer, 2003), 66.

33. Hidenori Niizawa, "On the Additionality of GHG Reduction," in *International Frameworks and Technological Strategies to Prevent Climate Change*, ed. Takamitsu Sawa (Tokyo/New York: Springer, 2003), 98.

34. See http://unfccc.int/Kyoto_protocol/mechanisms/clean_devel opment_mechanism.

35. The largest category by far of projects involves the energy industry, renewable and nonrenewable sources, totaling 759 certified between 2005 and 2007 alone. In this category of projects, 483, or 64 percent, are hosted by the four nations Brazil, China, India, and Mexico. In Africa, however, three projects are hosted in Morocco, six projects are hosted in South Africa, and one in Uganda.

Chapter Two

1. *Climate Change 2001; Impacts, Adaptation, and Vulnerability; Contribution of Working Group II to the Third Assessment Report of the Intergovernmental Panel on Climate Change* (approved in detail at the Sixth Session of IPCC Working Group II, Geneva, Switzerland, February 13–16, 2001) (Cambridge/New York: Cambridge University Press, 2001), 8.

2. Sir Nicholas Stern, *Stern Review: The Economics of Climate Change* (http://www.hm-treasury.gov.uk/stern_review_report.htm), 84.

3. Ibid.

4. *Climate Change 2007: Mitigation of Climate Change*, Contribution of Working Group III to the Fourth Assessment Report of the Intergovernmental Panel on Climate Change (Cambridge/New York: Cambridge University Press, 2007), "Summary for Policymakers," 15, topic 3.

5. Lorena Aguilar, "Women and Climate Change: Vulnerabilities and Adaptive Capacities," in 2009 *State of the World*, A Worldwatch Institute Report on Progress toward a Sustainable Society (New York and London: W. W. Norton, 2009), 59–52. The Global Gender and Climate Alliance was set up by the U.N. Development Programme, the International Union for the Conservation of Nature, the U.N. Environment Programme, and the Women's Environment and Development Organization.

6. Margaret M. Skutsch, "Protocols, Treaties, and Action: The 'Climate Change Process' Viewed through Gender Spectacles," in *Gender, Development, and Climate Change*, ed. Rachel Masika (Oxford: Oxfam GB, 2002), 35.

7. Ibid., 36.

8. Ibid.

9. Ibid., 37.

10. Irene Dankelman, "Climate Change: Learning from Gender Analysis and Women's Experiences of Organising for Sustainable Development," in *Gender, Development, and Climate Change*, 22.

11. Valerie Nelson, Kate Meadows, Terry Cannon, John Morton, and Adrienne Martin, "Uncertain Predictions, Invisible Impacts, and the Need to Mainstream Gender in Climate Change Adaptations," in *Gender, Development, and Climate Change*, 54.

12. Fatma Denton, "Climate Change Vulnerability, Impacts, and Adaptation: Why Does Gender Matter?" in *Gender, Development, and Climate Change*, 11.

13. Terry Cannon, "Gender and Climate Hazards in Bangladesh," in *Gender, Development, and Climate Change*, 45, 46.

14. Ibid., 46. This idea was developed in another chapter. "Cultural norms relating to the preservation of female honour through seclusion mean that women may delay leaving the home to seek refuge until it is too late. . . . Women are also less likely to learn to swim. An increase in flood frequency and intensity might thus increase female mortality" (Nelson et al., "Uncertain Predictions," 55). According to this source, however, more men died than women in Hurricane Mitch, which affected Honduras and Nicaragua, because ideas about masculinity encouraged risky heroic action.

15. Rosa Rivero Reyes, "Gendering Responses to El Niño in Rural Peru," in *Gender, Development, and Climate Change*, 60–64.

16. Andrew E. Dessler and Edward A. Parson, *The Science and Politics of Global Climate Change: A Guide to the Debate* (Cambridge/New York:: Cambridge University Press, 2006), 116.

17. For this treaty, see http://unfccc.int/resource/docs/conveng.pdf. Dessler and Parson's discussion of this principle can be found in *Science and Politics of Global Climate Change*, 13.

18. This particular formulation I owe to Takao Aiba and Tatsuyoshi Saijo, "The Kyoto Protocol and Global Environmental Strategies of the EU, the USA, and Japan: A Perspective from Japan," in *International Frameworks and Technological Strategies to Prevent Climate Change*, ed. Takamitsu Sawa (Tokyo/New York: Springer, 2003), 22.

19. I have yet to read a justification for this grandfathering by spokespeople for industrialized nations. The arena of Kyoto negotiations has been deeply affected by the reality of U.S. domestic politics. Since there is no basis for an effective treaty without U.S. collaboration, and since the U.S. Congress has been dominated by Republican concerns about the impact of reducing GHGs on economic growth, the question of justice in historic distribution patterns is not even on the table.

20. Hermann E. Ott and Wolfgang Sachs, "Ethical Aspects of Emission Trading" (paper to the WCC Consultation on "Equity and Emission Trading"), 11; published in *Ethics, Equity and International Negotiations on Climate Change*, ed. Luiz Pinguelli-Rosa and Mohan Munasinge (Cheltenham, UK/Northampton, Mass.: Elgar, 2002).

21. Centre for Science and Environment, "Equal Rights to the Atmosphere" (available from 41, Tughlakabad Institutional Area, New Delhi 110 062, India), 1. Another NGO representing this view at The Hague in November 2000 was Friends of the Earth International, who with several other organizations prepared the statement "Call for an Equitable Implementation and 'The Hague Mandate': Declaration on the Need for an Effective and Fair Agreement to Protect the Global Climate."

22. A Dutch government-sponsored study by International Project for Sustainable Energy Paths (ISEP) in 1989 calculated that to limit global warming to 2 degrees C by 2100, concentrations of GHGs should not exceed 430–450 ppm of CO_2 equivalent during the next century. This would mean a total of only 300 btC (billions ton carbon) can be released between 1985 and 2100, roughly 2.6 btC a year. Based on levels of population, the industrialized countries exhausted their quota in 1999. Developing countries could continue emitting CO_2 at 1986 levels until 2169. If the penalty is fifteen U.S. dollars per thousand tons of carbon over budget, and the accrued funds were distributed to nations whose emissions were below their per capita share, the top fifteen polluting nations would end up paying individual developing countries a total of twenty billion U.S. dollars annually. See Centre for Science and the Environment, "Equal Rights to the Atmosphere," 2.

23. This proposal was cited by Ambassador Raul A. Estrada-Oyuela in "Climate Change Mitigation and Equity" for the IPCC Second Regional Experts' Meeting on "Development, Equity, and Sustainability" in Havana, Cuba, February 23–25, 2000, 3.

24. See Nafisa Goga D'Souza, "Climate Change and Sustainability in the Indian Context," *Ecumenical Responses to Climate Change*, Papers from the WCC Consultation on "Climate Change and Sustainable Societies/Communities," Driebergen, The Netherlands, November 1996. Reprinted from *Ecumenical Review* 49, no. 2 (April 1997): 47. Also see Estrada, "Climate Change Mitigation," 6. Estrada shepherded the negotiations at the Kyoto meeting.

25. See Centre for Science and Environment, "Challenges Ahead," *Down to Earth*, Science and the Environment Fortnightly, March 31, 2000, 4. Also see "Call for an Equitable Implementation and 'The Hague Mandate': Declaration on the Need for an Effective and Fair Agreement to Protect the Global Climate," a statement prepared and endorsed by an international group of concerned organizations from the South and the North, for the Sixth Conference of the Parties to the Climate Change Convention (COP6) in The Hague, November 2000.

26. Centre for Science and Environment, "Boiling Point," *Down to Earth*, Science and the Environment Fortnightly, March 31, 2000, 3.

27. To prevent perverse incentives to countries to increase population size simply requires choosing a particular index year as the basis for rewarding emission rights. See Herman Verhagen and Jaap van der Sar, "United Air Fund: Towards a Just Distribution of the Consumption of the Atmosphere," in *The Earth's Atmosphere—Responsible Caring and Equitable Sharing for a Global Commons, Report, Statement and Background Papers from a Climate Change Consultation* sponsored by the World Council of Churches, David G. Hallman, Coordinator (Saskatoon, Canada, May 2000), 5.

28. These points are made by Ott and Sachs, "Ethical Aspects of Emissions Trading," 11–12. According to the Climate Action Newsletter *Eco*, published daily during the meeting at The Hague, the U.S. Department of Energy released a study in November 2000, completed by the five major U.S. government laboratories, which states that the United States can reach 75 percent of its Kyoto target at no cost to the economy. And yet the United States continues to be a leader in pushing for loopholes that could have the effect of canceling out its Kyoto commitment (http://www.igc.org/climate/8.1100.fossils.html).

29. One thoughtful statement supporting the implementation of the Kyoto Protocol but using no appeal to justice is that of Dr. Janet

Yellen, chair of the White House Council of Economic Advisers, in her "Statement on the Economics of the Kyoto Protocol" before the Committee on Agriculture, Nutrition, and Forestry of the U.S. Senate, March 5, 1998. She described the Clinton administration's reasons for insisting on "meaningful participation" from key developing countries before submitting the Protocol to the Senate. "Without the participation of developing economies, efforts by the industrialized countries to limit emissions will therefore not provide adequate protection from climate change. Second, developing country participation is crucial because it would permit relatively low-cost emissions reductions to be internationally recognized as a substitute for more expensive emissions reductions that might otherwise be achieved domestically by U.S. companies and those in other industrialized countries. Since greenhouse gas emissions have the same basic impact on the climate regardless of where they occur, emission reductions in developing countries have the same environmental benefit as reductions in the U.S. But these reductions are much less costly than reductions in the U.S. or in other developed nations, because of the very inefficient and carbon-intensive uses of energy in these countries today. It thus makes sense, from both an environmental and an economic perspective, to incorporate emissions reductions in developing countries into the international system." While Dr. Yellen's statement is an excellent attempt to describe fairly the Kyoto Protocol and the U.S. preference for flexibility mechanisms, it gives no assurance that industrialized nations intend to reduce emissions domestically. It is reasonable to read her statement and conclude that industrialized nations will attempt to get credit for all their targets without reducing emissions domestically. Statement available at http://search.epa.gov.

30. The "low-hanging fruit" concern is that developing countries should be wary of hosting CDM projects because they will focus on the easiest and least expensive projects, leaving only "high-hanging fruit"—more difficult projects—to the host country when it assumes its own GHG emissions abatement obligations. CDM projects might best be delayed until the host country can participate in JI (Joint Implementation) projects. "[T]here is indeed a case for this LHF argument, but not without qualifications. In particular, we found that both the cost of employing foreign technology and the extent of home technology improvements induced by the CDM experience must be at intermediate levels for the LHF argument to hold. Otherwise, it is in the interests of the host country (i) to stay away from the CDM/JI completely, (ii) to subject both LHF and HHF to JI, or (iii) to subject only LHF to JI." See Jiro Akita, "A Simple Model of CDM Low-Hanging Fruit," in *International*

Frameworks and Technological Strategies to Prevent Climate Change, ed. Takamitsu Sawa (Tokyo/New York: Springer, 2003), 14.

31. Estrada goes on to say, "Equity has different meanings in different contexts, equality has one single meaning. . . . In the field of the global commons like the atmosphere, the law is equality for every human being; but we use equity to moderate equality, to avoid equality, because equality is not acceptable for those who have been using a larger part of the atmosphere. . . . [W]e use the concept of equity because in the present context it is not possible to build a system on the basis of equality. Vested interests are strong enough and difficult to accommodate if we work towards equity, but they will block any progress if the target is equality." These comments appear in his address, "Climate Change Mitigation and Equity," to the IPCC Second Regional Experts' Meeting on "Development, Equity and Sustainability," Havana, Cuba, February 23–25, 2000, 1–2.

32. Warwick J. McKibben and Peter J. Wilcoxen, *Climate Change Policy after Kyoto: A Blueprint for a Realistic Approach* (Washington, D.C.: Brookings Institution Press, 2002), 79.

33. "Climate Change 'Can Be Tackled,'" BBC News, at http://news vote.bbc.co.uk/mpapps/pagetools/print/news.bbc.co.uk/2/hi/ (published May 4, 2007; accessed May 11, 2007).

34. J. Timmons Roberts and Bradley C. Parks, *A Climate of Injustice: Global Inequality, North–South Politics, and Climate Policy* (Cambridge, Mass./London: MIT Press, 2007), 30.

35. Ibid., 132.

36. Sir Nicholas Stern, *Stern Review: The Economics of Climate Change* (http://www.hm-treasury.gov.uk/IndependentReviews/Sternreview economicsclimatechange/stern reviewindex.cfm), p. 169.

37. Roberts and Parks, *Climate of Injustice*, 36.

38. Secretary of State Madeleine K. Albright, "Statement before the International Relations Committee," Washington, D.C., February 12, 1998. Accessible at http://www.fas.org/asmp/resources/govern/fy99 albright.html (accessed May 14, 2007).

39. McKibben and Wilcoxen, *Climate Change Policy after Kyoto*, 68–69, emphasis added.

40. Hermann E. Ott and Wolfgang Sachs, "Ethical Aspects of Emission Trading" (paper to the WCC Consultation on "Equity and Emission Trading"), 11; published in *Ethics, Equity and International Negotiations on Climate Change*, ed. Luiz Pinguelli-Rosa and Mohan Munasinge (Cheltenham, UK/Northampton, Mass.: Elgar, 2002).

41. Centre for Science and Environment, "Equal Rights to the Atmosphere," 1. Also see Roberts and Parks, *Climate of Injustice*, 144–45.

42. Roberts and Parks, *Climate of Injustice,* 146–50.

43. Ibid., 143.

44. Ibid., 150. See also José D. G. Miguez, "Equity, Responsibility and Climate Change," in *Ethics, Equity and International Negotiations on Climate Change,* ed. Luiz Pinguelli-Rosa and Mohan Munasinge (Cheltenham, UK/Northampton, Mass.: Elgar, 2002), 7–35.

45. T. Barker, I. Bashmakov, L. Bernstein, et al., "Technical Summary," in *Climate Change 2007: Mitigation of Climate Change,* Contribution of Working Group III to the Fourth Assessment Report of the Intergovernmental Panel on Climate Change (Cambridge/New York: Cambridge University Press, 2007), 89.

46. Ibid., 47.

Chapter Three

1. See, as a recent example, the WCC address to the conference in Bali, Indonesia, Friday, December 14, 2007. The statement is accessible at http://www.oikoumene.org/?id=5323.

2. Intergovernmental Panel on Climate Change Special Report on Emissions Scenarios, Chapter 1, "Background and Overview," and particularly 1.2, "What Are Scenarios?" and 1.7.2, "Narrative Storylines and Scenario Quantifications." The report can be found online at http://www.grida.no/climate/ipcc/emission/030.htm. The Special Report has been published as Nebojšs Nakićenović et al., *Special Report on Emissions Scenarios: A Special Report of Working Group III of the Intergovernmental Panel on Climate Change* (Cambridge/New York:: Cambridge University Press, 2000); this background can be found on p. 3. The fifth assessment will not use the same factors to distinguish the scenarios. "The Panel agreed at its 28th Session in Budapest (April 2008) to organize the new assessment work around a revised set of scenarios of socio-economic, climate, and environmental conditions. Instead of resulting from population projections and development hypotheses, as was the case up to now, they are based on a range of possible evolution patterns for the atmospheric concentration of greenhouse gases ('representative concentration pathways'), which will serve simultaneously as benchmarks for the development of new climate model simulations and targets for the development of emissions and socio-economic scenarios." http://www.ipcc.ch/popup_scenarios.htm.

3. The image can be found in the IPCC Special Report on Emissions Scenarios, 1.7.2, "Narrative Storylines and Scenario Quantifications," figs. 1–4. Also see Nakićenović et al., *Special Report,* 28.

4. In the IPCC Special Report on Emissions Scenarios, one finds the declaration, "While the writing team as a whole has no preference for any of these scenarios, and has no judgment as to the probability or desirability of different scenarios, the open process and initial reactions to draft versions of this report show that individuals and interest groups do have such judgments. The writing team hopes that this will stimulate an open discussion in the policy making arena about potential futures and choices that can be made in the context of climate change response." See the IPCC Special Report on Emissions Scenarios, 6.4, "Summary and Conclusions."

5. T. Barker, I. Bashmakov, L. Bernstein, et al., "Technical Summary," in *Climate Change 2007: Mitigation of Climate Change. Contribution of Working Group III to the Fourth Assessment Report of the Intergovernmental Panel on Climate Change* (Cambridge/New York: Cambridge University Press, 2007), 37.

6. The image of the Council of All Beings is evocative without further explanation. It is associated with a series of rituals created by John Seed and Joanna Macy to allow other life forms to speak through us. For the philosophy grounding the Council rituals, see Joanna Macy, "The Ecological Self: Postmodern Ground for Right Action," in Mary Heather MacKinnon and Moni McIntyre, *Readings in Ecology and Feminist Theology* (Kansas City: Sheed and Ward, 1995), 259–69.

7. See http://www.grida.no/climate/ipcc/emission/101.htm.

8. This study was provided staff support by the United Nations Environment Programme (UNEP); the Food and Agriculture Organization of the United Nations, Italy; the Institute of Economic Growth, India; the Meridian Institute, United States; Scientific Committee on Problems of the Environment (SCOPE), France; and seven other national research agencies. The breadth of participation in doing the assessment is worth noting: approximately 1,360 experts from ninety-five countries were involved as authors of the assessment reports, as participants in the subglobal assessments, or as members of the Board of Review Editors. The report was released in January 2006 by Island Press, Washington, D.C. The Millennium Assessment Report (MAR) used and developed the descriptions of the IPCC SRES scenarios, as well as two other scenario efforts. The Millennium Assessment is available at www.millennium assessment.org/.

9. Millennium Assessment Report, 226–27.

10. IPCC Special Report on Emissions Scenarios, chapter 4, 4.3.1, "A1 Storyline and Scenario Family." Or see Nakićenović et al., *Special Report*, 179–80.

11. Millennium Ecosystem Assessment, *Ecosystems and Human Well-Being*, vol. 2, chapter 5, 129–32 (www.millenniumassessment.org/).

12. Sir Nicholas Stern, *Stern Review: The Economics of Climate Change* (http://www.hm-treasury.gov.uk/IndependentReviews/Sternreview economicsclimatechange/stern reviewindex.cfm), 181.

13. IPCC Special Report on Emissions Scenarios, 4.3.2; or see Nakićenović et al., *Special Report*, 180–81.

14. IPCC Special Report on Emissions Scenarios, 4.4.7.3, "A2 Scenarios"; or see Nakićenović et al., *Special Report*, 214.

15. Millennium Ecosystem Assessment, *Ecosystems and Human Well-Being*, 133–34.

16. Ibid., 226.

17. IPCC Special Report on Emissions Scenarios, 4.4.4.5, "B1 Scenarios"; or see Nakićenović et al., *Special Report*, 200.

18. It is assumed in this scenario that subsidies on coal for generation of electricity are removed entirely. But the modeling does not distinguish between nuclear, solar, or wind power generation technologies, according to IPCC Special Report on Emissions Scenarios, 4.4.7.4, "B1 Scenarios"; or see Nakićenović et al., *Special Report*, 214.

19. IPCC Special Report on Emissions Scenarios, 4.4.4.5, "B1 Scenarios"; or see Nakićenović et al., *Special Report*, 200.

20. Millennium Ecosystem Assessment, *Ecosystems and Human Well-Being*, 2:135–37.

21. IPCC Special Report on Emissions Scenarios, 4.4.7.5, "B2 Scenarios"; or see Nakićenović et al., *Special Report*, 215.

22. Millennium Ecosystem Assessment, *Ecosystems and Human Well-Being*, 276.

23. Ibid., 134–35.

24. Bonnie B. Burgess, *Fate of the Wild: The Endangered Species Act and the Future of Biodiversity* (Athens, Ga. and London: University of Georgia Press, 2001), 29–30.

25. Martin Parry, Osvaldo Canziani, Jean Palutikof, et al., "Technical Summary," Working Group II Fourth Assessment, in *Climate Change 2007*, 34.

26. Mary Ashley, "Catholic Moral Reasoning: An Evaluation in Relation to Global Climate Change" (M.A. thesis, Graduate Theological Union, Berkeley, Calif., 2007).

27. Carol J. Manahan, "The Moral Economy of Corn: Starlink and the Ethics of Resistance" (Ph.D. diss., Graduate Theological Union, Berkeley, Calif., 2006), particularly chap. 4.

28. Mark Roseland and Lena Soots, "Strengthening Local Economies," in Worldwatch Institute, *State of the World 2007: Our Urban Future* (New York/London: W. W. Norton, 2007), 169.

Chapter Four

1. Some recent efforts to describe how Christians do or should use biblical texts in contemporary ethics include Thomas W. Ogletree, *The Use of the Bible in Christian Ethics: A Constructive Essay* (Philadelphia: Fortress, 1983); Allen Verhey, *The Great Reversal, Ethics and the New Testament* (Grand Rapids: Eerdmans, 1984); William C. Spohn, *Go and Do Likewise: Jesus and Ethics* (New York: Continuum, 2006); Jeffrey S. Siker, *Scripture and Ethics, Twentieth-Century Portraits* (New York/Oxford: Oxford University Press, 1995); Brian K. Blount, *Then the Whisper Put on Flesh: New Testament Ethics in an African American Context* (Nashville: Abingdon, 2001); Renita J. Weems, *Battered Love: Marriage, Sex, and Violence in the Hebrew Prophets*, Overtures to Biblical Theology (Minneapolis: Fortress Press, 1995); Richard B. Hays, *The Moral Vision of the New Testament: Community, Cross, New Creation. A Contemporary Introduction to New Testament Ethics* (San Francisco: HarperSanFrancisco, 1996); Charles H. Cosgrove, *Appealing to Scripture in Moral Debate: Five Hermeneutical Rules* (Grand Rapids: Eerdmans, 2002). On this topic, our work is never done.

2. Eung Chun Park, *Either Jew or Gentile: Paul's Unfolding Theology of Inclusivity* (Louisville: Westminster John Knox, 2003), 26.

3. L. William Countryman, *Biblical Authority or Biblical Tyranny? Scripture and the Christian Pilgrimage* (Philadelphia: Fortress Press, 1981), 81.

4. Bruce J. Malina has often warned against these twin dangers; see, for instance, his *The Social Gospel of Jesus: The Kingdom of God in Mediterranean Perspective* (Minneapolis: Fortress Press, 2001).

5. Countryman, *Biblical Authority*.

6. Fernando F. Segovia, "Toward a Hermeneutics of the Diaspora: A Hermeneutics of Otherness and Engagement," in *Reading from This Place*, vol. 1, *Social Location and Biblical Interpretation in the United States*, ed. Fernando F. Segovia and Mary Ann Tolbert (Minneapolis: Fortress Press, 1995), 68.

7. Biblical quotations are according to the New Revised Standard Version.

8. Malina, *Social Gospel of Jesus*, 109.

9. One recent edition of Max Weber's discussion of this phenomenon is *The Protestant Ethic and the Spirit of Capitalism* (Los Angeles: Roxbury, 1996 and later editions).

10. Bruce J. Malina and John J. Pilch, *Social-Science Commentary on the Letters of Paul*, Social Science Commentary (Minneapolis: Fortress Press, 2006), 7.

11. Ibid., 375.

12. Marvin L. Chaney "Pluralism in Text and Context: Some Reflections on a Hermeneutic of Dynamic Analogy between Biblical Israel and Historical Korea," in *Biblical Israel through an Agrarian Lens: Essays on Religion and Society in Old Testament History, Literature and Interpretation*, ed. Taek Joo Woo (Seoul, Korea: Handl, 2007), 19. The pagination is for the English language article, not the Korean-language publication.

13. Ibid., 23.

14. Ibid., 26.

15. Hays, *Moral Vision*.

16. Jack Bartlett Rogers, *Jesus, the Bible, and Homosexuality: Explode the Myths, Heal the Church* (Louisville: Westminster John Knox, 2006), 44–65.

17. Such awareness is what Segovia calls the second dimension of intercultural criticism ("Toward a Hermeneutics of the Diaspora," 69).

18. Zachary Coile, "Staff at EPA Backed State on Reducing Car Emissions," *San Francisco Chronicle*, December 21, 2007, A1, 21.

19. Zachary Coile, "EPA Chief Sits and Takes His Punishment," *San Francisco Chronicle*, January 25, 2008, A4.

20. Mark Z. Jacobson, "EPA's Own Study Argues for California Waiver," *San Francisco Chronicle*, March 3, 2008, B5.

21. Matthew B. Stannard, "EPA Lets State Get Tougher on New Vehicles," *San Francisco Chronicle*, July 1, 2009, A1, A8.

22. Walter G. Muelder, *Moral Law in Christian Social Ethics* (Richmond: John Knox, 1966), 152.

23. Denis Edwards, *Jesus the Wisdom of God: An Ecological Theology*, Ecology and Justice (Maryknoll, N.Y.: Orbis, 1995), esp. 33–37, for identification of these hymns.

24. Antoinette Clark Wire, "The God of Jesus in the Gospel Sayings Source," in *Reading from This Place*, vol. 1, *Social Location and Biblical Interpretation in the United States*, ed. Fernando F. Segovia and Mary Ann Tolbert (Minneapolis: Fortress Press, 1995), 279. For instances of Jesus describing Wisdom as mother or sender of prophets, see Luke 7:35; 11:49; and 13:34//Matthew 23:37-39. There is, of course, a real possibility that while in the final redaction of the Gospels of Matthew and Luke there is no conflict between Jesus the sage and Jesus the prophet, within the Q source there may be two somewhat different layers of tradition that depicted Jesus as either sage or prophet. Scholars such as John S.

Kloppenborg, John Dominic Crossan, Burton Mack, and Helmut Koester discuss this possibility.

25. See Richard A. Horsley, *Galilee: History, Politics, People* (Valley Forge, Pa.: Trinity Press International, 1995), for reasons why it may be historically anachronistic to refer to Jesus as a Jew (he was Galilean rather than Judean), to refer to Judaism as a common identity of Judeans and Galileans, or to refer to Judaism and Christianity as "religions" distinct from political-economic phenomena prior to the third century C.E.

26. Weems, *Battered Love*, 103–4.

Chapter Five

1. I think particularly of Paula Fredriksen in two books, *Jesus of Nazareth, King of the Jews: A Jewish Life and the Emergence of Christianity* (New York: Knopf, 1999), and *From Jesus to Christ: The Origins of the New Testament Images of Jesus* (New Haven: Yale University Press, 1988); William Herzog in two books, *Jesus, Justice, and the Reign of God: A Ministry of Liberation* (Louisville: Westminster John Knox, 2000), and *Parables as Subversive Speech: Jesus as Pedagogue of the Oppressed* (Louisville: Westminster John Knox, 1994); Douglas E. Oakman, *Jesus and the Economic Questions of His Day*, Studies in the Bible and Early Christianity 8 (Lewiston, N.Y.: Edwin Mellen, 1986); Bruce J. Malina, *The Social Gospel of Jesus: The Kingdom of God in Mediterranean Perspective* (Minneapolis: Fortress Press, 2000); N. T. Wright, *Christian Origins and the Question of God*, vol. 2, *Jesus and the Victory of God* (Minneapolis: Fortress Press, 1996).

2. I owe this formulation to Bill Herzog in his *Jesus, Justice, and the Reign of God*, 124–32.

3. For an argument that Jesus may not have been a peasant artisan, but an outcast of Hasmonean heritage, see Marianne Sawicki, *Crossing Galilee: Architectures of Contact in the Occupied Land of Jesus* (Harrisburg, Pa.: Trinity Press International, 2000), 144, 186, 192–97.

4. I use two sources to draw this history of the two regions in relation to the temple: Richard A. Horsley, *Galilee: History, Politics, People* (Valley Forge, Pa.: Trinity Press International, 1995), 19–61; and Sawicki, *Crossing Galilee*, 82–147.

5. Horsley, *Galilee*, 28–29.

6. Sawicki, *Crossing Galilee*, 172.

7. Sawicki (ibid., 137–38) wonders whether Mary the mother of Jesus was the daughter of a Hasmonean administrator, and perhaps was

present in Sepphoris when Roman soldiers conquered it in 4 B.C.E. John the Baptist's parents seem to have been Hasmonean in heritage also.

8. Herzog, *Jesus, Justice, and the Reign of God*, 103.

9. Fredriksen, *Jesus of Nazareth*, 52.

10. Horsley (*Galilee*, 197), focusing on the distinctive history of Galilee as opposed to Judea, wonders how much of the Deuteronomic code was part of Torah instruction for Galilean villagers, and therefore how much of the purity code was in their tradition. "Galilee had been independent of the Monarchic or second-temple state in Jerusalem from before the time of the 'Deuteronomic reform' of the seventh century B.C.E., coming back under Jerusalem control only at the end of the second-temple period."

11. Fredriksen, *Jesus of Nazareth*, 53.

12. For a succinct version of Fredriksen's argument, see her "Go, show yourself to the priest, and offer for your cleansing what Moses commanded. (MK 1:44): Jesus, Purity, and the Christian Study of Judaism," at www.bu.edu/religion/faculty/Fredriksen/purity.html.

13. It was because they perceived, along with Rome, the threat implied in Jesus' preaching the imminent coming of the kingdom of God (ibid.).

14. Fredriksen understands the "incident" at the temple is this way: Jesus was not "cleansing" the temple of moneychangers, because they were necessary for foreign and all other travelers who needed to purchase their sacrifices. The incident was a gesture symbolizing God's destruction of this temple so that, at the end of the age, another would be built, not with human hands. This gesture would then be consistent with prophecies concerning the restoration of Israel under the rule of God (ibid.).

15. Sawicki, *Crossing Galilee*, 54.

16. Ibid., 53.

17. This history of the temple priesthood is primarily based on Fredriksen, *Jesus of Nazareth*, 165–81. Herzog uses a similar analysis.

18. Herzog, *Jesus, Justice, and the Reign of God*, 121. Here Herzog is using the work of Sheldon Isenberg, "Power through Temple and Torah in Greco-Roman Palestine," in *Christianity, Judaism, and Other Greco-Roman Cults: Studies for Morton Smith at Sixty*, Part 2, *Early Christianity*, ed. Jacob Neusner, Studies in Judaism in Late Antiquity 12 (Leiden: Brill, 1975), 24–52.

19. A good social history of the steward can be found in Herzog, *Parables as Subversive Speech*, 53–73, 233–58.

20. Herzog (ibid., 79–97) is the source of this interpretation of the parable of the laborers in the vineyard.

21. Herzog (ibid., 233–58) is the source of this interpretation of the parable of the dishonest steward.

22. Herzog, *Jesus, Justice, and the Reign of God*, 123. Here Herzog uses the work of Sean Freyne, *Galilee from Alexander the Great to Hadrean, 323 BCE to 135 CE* (Notre Dame, Ind.: University of Notre Dame Press, 1980), to make this connection between the temple and the land.

23. For the interpretation of the story of Jesus healing the paralytic, see Herzog, *Jesus, Justice, and the Reign of God*, 124–33.

24. Ibid., 156–57. In this discussion of the two codes of the Torah, Herzog is using the analysis of Fernando Belo, *A Materialist Reading of the Gospel of Mark*, trans. Matthew J. O'Connell (Maryknoll, N.Y.: Orbis, 1981).

25. Herzog, *Jesus, Justice, and the Reign of God*, 157.

26. Ibid., 158.

27. See ibid., 158–67, for the interpretation of this Markan passage.

28. Sawicki, *Crossing Galilee*, 145.

29. Ibid., 178.

Chapter Six

1. See particularly John P. Meier, *A Marginal Jew: Rethinking the Historical Jesus*, vol 2, *Mentor, Message, and Miracles*, Anchor Bible Reference Library (New York: Doubleday, 1994). Other authors include Paula Fredriksen, *From Jesus to Christ: The Origins of the New Testament Images of Jesus* (New Haven: Yale University Press, 1988); idem, *Jesus of Nazareth, King of the Jews: A Jewish Life and the Emergence of Christianity* (New York: Knopf, 1999); William R. Herzog, *Parables as Subversive Speech: Jesus as Pedagogue of the Oppressed* (Louisville: Westminster John Knox, 1994); idem, *Jesus, Justice, and the Reign of God: A Ministry of Liberation* (Louisville: Westminster John Knox, 2000); Marianne Sawicki, *Crossing Galilee: Architectures of Contact in the Occupied Land of Jesus* (Harrisburg, Pa.: Trinity Press International, 2000); Bruce J. Malina, *The Social Gospel of Jesus: The Kingdom of God in Mediterranean Perspective* (Minneapolis: Fortress Press, 2000).

2. This summary is of material that can be found in Meier, *Mentor, Message, and Miracles*, 237–53.

3. Ibid., 239.

4. Richard A. Horsley (*Galilee: History, Politics, People* [Valley Forge, Pa.: Trinity Press International, 1995], 65) recounts this period of Palestine's history, as does Sawicki, *Crossing Galilee*, 82–85, 135–43.

5. Meier, *Mentor, Message, and Miracles*, 1041–42.

6. I am relying here on Richard A. Horsley, "Popular Messianic Movements around the Time of Jesus," *Catholic Biblical Quarterly* 46, no. 3 (1984): 471–95, here 472–83.

7. Ibid., 483–87.

8. Ibid., 488–90.

9. Fredriksen, *From Jesus to Christ*, 35.

10. Ibid., 169.

11. Ibid., 167.

12. For a close reading of the Acts of the Apostles and the letters of Paul as source material, along with other sources, to expose the conflict within the early churches regarding the gospel of circumcision and the gospel of uncircumcision, see Eung Chun Park, *Either Jew or Gentile: Paul's Unfolding Theology of Inclusivity* (Louisville: Westminster John Knox, 2003).

13. There is no sense denying the reality of apocalypses. Anyone familiar with the likely consequences of unabated climate change has a sense of the imminence of an apocalypse. Dresden, Hiroshima, Nagasaki, Bosnia, and Iraq have lived and died through apocalypses. I cannot believe these apocalypses are the will of God or the revelation of God's purposes for this earth. They are the monstrous evil we do to each other.

14. In this regard I differ from my late colleague, William Spohn, *Go and Do Likewise: Jesus and Ethics* (New York: Continuum, 1999), 146. In general terms, his book is an effort to draw out how character/virtue ethics is the most appropriate way to approach the Scriptures and examine the story of Jesus. And while recognizing Paul's dramatic healing and moral transformation, Spohn wrote that most Christians experience the more pedestrian route of Peter and the other disciples, whose (moral) blindness is not total and who do not recover their (moral) sight in a miraculous instant. Spohn deepened the discussion of how the New Testament enriches the moral life of Christians: reading the New Testament in community, engaging in liturgical practices, and deepening spirituality do have an effect on Christians' "moral psychology"—our imaginations, emotions, perceptions, convictions, and actions. It seems to me, however, that there is some irony in Spohn's agreement with Paul's focus on the cross and the resurrection as the "master paradigm" of the Christian moral life. If I read him correctly, he agreed with Paul's atonement theology, which he characterized in this way: "The real oppressor of Israel was not Rome but the forces of cosmic evil. God defeated evil not by violent resistance but by overcoming it in the death of Jesus. He absorbed the full impact of evil in his own body, and it destroyed him. But God proved faithful to his servant and raised him from the dead. Everything must be

considered in reference to this event *because it has inaugurated the final era of history*" (p. 146, emphasis added). The questions that emerged for me as I read what I view as a wise book is this: What are the ecological consequences of viewing God's actions through Christ as ensuring a limited future for the earth? And can this interpretation of atonement coexist with a serious review of the social world of Jesus' day, and therefore the layers of meaning that inhabit biblical texts?

15. Wisdom counsels that in the social arena no one really exercises control, though autocrats try and, to a certain degree at least for a time, may succeed. Obviously I am not advocating for autocratic control. Rather, I refer to exercising choice in social policy that decreases industrialized nations' use of fossil fuel and increases reliance on renewable energy sources.

16. Sawicki, *Crossing Galilee*, 174.

17. Ibid., 179.

18. Ibid., 177–78.

19. Antoinette Clark Wire develops the reason for translating *kingdom* as "inheritance" in "The God of Jesus in the Gospel Sayings Source," in *Reading from This Place*, vol. 1, *Social Location and Biblical Interpretation in the United States*, ed. Fernando F. Segovia and Mary Ann Tolbert (Minneapolis: Fortress Press, 1995), 277–303, here 281, and more fully in "Full Communion of Lutheran and Reformed Churches in Light of Jesus' Story" in Harding Meyer and Antoinette Clark Wire, *Lutheran-Reformed Theological Reflections on Full Communion*, Occasional Papers contributing to the 1997 decisions, Department for Ecumenical Affairs, Evangelical Lutheran Church in America, 15–18.

20. Wire, "God of Jesus in the Gospel Sayings Source," 281.

21. For a review of the historical sources, see Horsley, "Popular Messianic Movements," 471–95.

22. My source for this treatment of the three growth parables is Douglas E. Oakman, *Jesus and the Economic Questions of His Day*, Studies in the Bible and Early Christianity 8 (Lewiston, N.Y.: Edwin Mellen, 1986), chap. 3.

23. A scholar who develops this intrinsic relationship is V. J. John, "Nature Images in the Nature Parables of Mark's Gospel" (Th.D., diss., Serampore College, Bangalore, India, 2000). John uses Oakman's work along with a range of other exegetes. Also see V. J. John, "Towards a Biblical Understanding of Ecology: Re-Reading the Agricultural Parables of Jesus," in *Theologies and Cultures*, IV, #1, June, 2007, 119–46.

24. John, "Nature Images," chap. 4.

25. Herzog, *Jesus, Justice, and the Reign of God*, 199.

Chapter Seven

1. Richard A. Horsley, "Rhetoric and Empire—and 1 Corinthians," in *Paul and Politics: Ekklesia, Israel, Imperium, and Interpretation. Essays in Honor of Krister Stendahl,* ed. Richard A. Horsley (Harrisburg, Pa.: Trinity Press International, 2000), 72–102, here 75–82. In the same volume, see also Sheila Briggs, "Paul on Bondage and Freedom in Imperial Society," 110–23, here 110.

2. S. R. F. Price, "Rituals and Power," in *Paul and Empire: Religion and Power in Roman Imperial Society,* ed. Richard A. Horsley (Harrisburg, Pa.: Trinity Press International, 1997), 47–71, here 52–71.

3. Ibid., 59.

4. Bruce J. Malina and John J. Pilch, *Social-Science Commentary on the Letters of Paul,* Social Science Commentary (Minneapolis: Fortress Press, 2006), 260–61.

5. Ibid., 261.

6. Neil Elliott, *Liberating Paul: The Justice of God and the Politics of the Apostle,* Bible and Liberation Series (Maryknoll, N.Y.: Orbis, 1994), 25–54.

7. Ibid., 25, 27. The assessment that 1 Corinthians 14:33b-36 is an interpolation is shared by Robert Jewett, "Response: Exegetical Support from Romans and Other Letters," in Horsley, *Paul and Politics,* 58–71, here 59. This view is challenged by Elisabeth Schüssler Fiorenza, *In Memory of Her: A Feminist Theological Reconstruction of Christian Origins* (New York: Crossroad, 1983), 233.

8. Elliott, *Liberating Paul,* 25, 27, 214–26.

9. According to Elliott (*Liberating Paul,* 29–30), "We must recognize that the Paul who speaks to us in the New Testament as a whole is an artificial composite, resulting in part from a campaign of deliberate revision of the memory of Paul." The pseudepigraphical letters, written under Paul's name by others, are deliberate alterations of the received tradition (E. Elizabeth Johnson) and are forgeries. They were adopted into the canon under the misconception that they actually were by Paul.

10. Schüssler Fiorenza, *In Memory of Her,* 56; and Elliott, *Liberating Paul,* 28–31.

11. Schüssler Fiorenza, *In Memory of Her,* 183.

12. Elliott, *Liberating Paul,* 35.

13. The reading of the letter that emphasizes Paul's appeal to conscience rather than his own power to command, thus opening the door to moral response, is exemplified by Lloyd A. Lewis, "Philemon," in *True to Our Native Land: An African American New Testament Commentary,* ed.

Brian K. Blount (Minneapolis: Fortress Press, 2007), 437–42; and John Dominic Crossan, *God and Empire: Jesus against Rome, Then and Now* (San Francisco: HarperSanFrancisco, 2007), 158–64.

14. Elliott, *Liberating Paul*, 35–49.

15. Malina and Pilch, *Social-Science Commentary*, 279–80.

16. Elliott, *Liberating Paul*, 99.

17. Ibid., 122–29.

18. Schüssler Fiorenza, *In Memory of Her*, 130.

19. Neil Elliott, "The Anti-Imperial Message of the Cross," in Horsley, *Paul and Empire*, 167–83, here 183.

20. Elisabeth Schüssler Fiorenza, *The Power of the Word: Scripture and the Rhetoric of Empire* (Minneapolis: Fortress Press, 2007), 71. Schüssler Fiorenza notes that the classical Greek institution of democracy in theory promised freedom and equality to all its citizens, but in practice granted such rights only to imperial, elite, propertied, educated male heads of household by restricting full citizenship to them. Hence, the *ekklēsia* as the radical democratic congress of citizen subjects has never been fully realized (p. 72).

21. Richard A. Horsley, "Introduction to Part 4, Building an Alternative Society," in Horsley, *Paul and Empire*, 206–14, here 208.

22. Ibid., 208.

23. Allen Dwight Callahan, "Paul, Ekklesia, and Emancipation in Corinth," in Horsley, *Paul and Politics*, 216–23, here 220–21.

24. N. T. Wright, "Paul's Gospel and Caesar's Empire," in Horsley, *Paul and Politics*, 160–83, here 182.

25. Horsley, "Rhetoric and Empire," 97.

26. Richard A. Horsley, "1 Corinthians: A Case Study of Paul's Assembly as an Alternative Society," in Horsley, *Paul and Empire*, 242–52, here 251.

27. Sze-kar Wan, "Collection for the Saints as Anticolonial Act: Implications of Paul's Ethnic Reconstruction," in Horsley, *Paul and Politics*, 191–215, here 192.

28. Callahan, "Paul, Ekklesia," 221.

29. Horsley, "1 Corinthians: A Case Study," 251.

30. Wan, "Collection," 207.

31. Ibid., 214–15.

32. Dieter Georgi, "God Turned Upside Down," in Horsley, *Paul and Empire*, 148–57, here 157.

33. Wright, "Paul's Gospel and Caesar's Empire," 181.

34. Ibid., 182.

35. Schüssler Fiorenza, *Power of the Word*, 152–56, 180.

36. Antoinette Clark Wire, *The Corinthian Women Prophets: A Reconstruction through Paul's Rhetoric* (Minneapolis: Fortress Press, 1990), 62.

37. Ibid., 67.

38. Ibid., 187.

39. I have not been able to find this image in Wire's text. It was one she used in a class that she and I taught together on New Testament and Feminist Ethics, at the Graduate Theological Union (a consortium that includes San Francisco Theological Seminary) in Spring 2004.

40. Cynthia Briggs Kittredge, "Corinthian Women Prophets and Paul's Argumentation in 1 Corinthians," in Horsley, *Paul and Politics*, 103–9.

41. Wire, *Corinthian Women Prophets*, 139.

42. Ibid., 156.

43. Horsley, "Rhetoric and Empire," 91–92, 93.

44. Ephesians 5:22-23; Colossians 3:18-19; 1 Timothy 2:8-15; Titus 2:4-5; 1 Peter 3:1-7. These texts may share a common origin with 1 Corinthians 11:3-6 and 14:34-35—a "Paulinist" who appeals to the creation account in Genesis 2 and the fall of humankind in Genesis 3 to construct the arguments about the place of women. In so doing, the "Paulinist" is using the authority of Paul to neutralize Paul's more egalitarian positions. For a discussion of this possibility, see Demetrius K. Williams, *An End to This Strife: The Politics of Gender in African American Churches* (Minneapolis: Fortress Press, 2004), 54–58.

45. The household code was "authorized" by Aristotle in *The Politics* and by the Greco-Roman or Jewish-Hellenistic philosophical schools of the first century C.E., reflecting the belief that, although equality is a social value, people are defined by their natures: the male is by nature better suited to command and is therefore the natural ruler; the female is the natural subject. These differences in essence must be properly structured and ordered to maintain harmony in the household, which is a microcosm of the state. The code was an ethic of the propertied classes, who had slaves. Colossians 3:23 is an expansion of the code's third pair, slave–master. Colossians makes the Greco-Roman ethic for slaves "Christian." Schüssler Fiorenza notes that this interpretation of the baptismal formula in Galatians 3:28 did not appear until the last third of the first century. "It is found in only one segment of early Christianity, the post-Pauline tradition, and had no impact on the Jesus traditions." See her discussion of the household code in *In Memory of Her*, 253–54.

46. Elisabeth Schüssler Fiorenza, *Bread Not Stone: The Challenge of Feminist Biblical Interpretation* (Boston: Beacon, 1984), 71.

47. Williams, *End to This Strife*, 60.

48. Clarice J. Martin, "The Haustafeln (Household Codes) in African American Biblical Interpretation: 'Free Slaves' and 'Subordinate Women,'" in *Stony the Road We Trod: African American Biblical Interpretation*, ed. Cain Hope Felder (Minneapolis: Fortress Press, 1991), 210. Martin attributes this definition to Gerd Theissen, who took the phrase "love patriarchalism" from Ernst Troeltsch.

49. Schüssler Fiorenza, *In Memory of Her*, 256–57.

50. Malina and Pilch, *Social-Science Commentary*, 7.

51. Ibid., 264.

52. Ibid., 273. In their substantial commentary on Romans 1:24-27, Malina and Pilch trace the language of "according to nature" to the Roman natural law. It had very little relationship to what "moderns" consider natural as described by the natural sciences. See pp. 229–31.

53. Ibid., 274.

54. Ibid., 9.

55. Malina and Pilch (*Social-Science Commentary*, 29) describe the Talmud as "an extensive compilation of opinions about the Torah."

56. Malina and Pilch, *Social-Science Commentary*, 14–15.

57. Ibid., 236.

58. Ibid., 38.

59. Ibid., 67.

60. Ibid., 51. Malina and Pilch reference these texts regarding the restoration of Israel: Isaiah 2; Ezekiel 30; 34; 36; Joel 2:2; 3:4; 4:15; Micah 1:2-3; Zephaniah 1:15; Zechariah 14.

Chapter Eight

1. Conversation with Dr. Eugene Eung Chun Park, professor of New Testament at San Francisco Theological Seminary, March 2008.

2. See William L. Holladay, *The Psalms through Three Thousand Years: A Prayerbook of a Cloud of Witnesses* (Minneapolis: Fortress Press, 1993), 39–40. The Egyptian hymn is the Hymn to the Aton. "The Aton" in Egypt was the sun disk, the source of life, and the hymn stems from the reign of Akh-en-Aton (also spelled Ikhnaton or Akhenaten). Holladay believes that the Egyptian material may have been mediated through Phoenicia. However this material entered into the liturgical life of Israel, it is likely to have done so in the period of Solomon, or at least before the Babylonian exile. After the exile, the Jewish community was less open to foreign influences.

3. Bruce J. Malina and John J. Pilch, *Social-Science Commentary on the Letters of Paul*, Social Science Commentary (Minneapolis: Fortress Press, 2006), 77, 260.

4. Edgar W. Conrad, "Messengers in the Sky," in Norman C. Habel, ed., *Readings from the Perspective of Earth* (Sheffield and Cleveland: Pilgrim, 2000), 86. Conrad notes that it was John Calvin who argued against translating a Hebrew word as "angels" when it should be translated as "messenger," and that prophets were often called messengers in the Hebrew Bible.

5. Randolph E. Schmid, "CO_2 in Air Growing Faster Than Expected," *San Francisco Chronicle*, October 23, 2007, A13.

6. This standard is taken from David Hallman, "Ecumenical Responses to Climate Change: A Summary of the History and Dynamics of Ecumenical Involvement in the Issue of Climate Change," in *Ecumenical Responses to Climate Change*, Papers from the World Council of Churches Consultation on "Climate Change and Sustainable Societies/Communities," in Driebergen, The Netherlands, November 1996, 11.

7. David Malin Roodman, *Paying the Piper: Subsidies, Politics, and the Environment*, Worldwatch Paper 133 (Washington, D.C.: Worldwatch Institute, 1996), 39.

8. These topics are the primary contents of Christopher Flavin and Seth Dunn's book, *Rising Sun, Gathering Winds: Policies to Stabilize the Climate and Strengthen Economies*, Worldwatch Paper 138 (Washington, D.C.: Worldwatch Institute, 1997).

9. Angie Sutton, "Harvesting the Wind," *Kansas Living, A Publication of Kansas Farm Bureau* [Manhattan, Kans.] (Summer 2007): 18–20.

10. Charles Burress, "The Deadly Toll of Wind Power," *San Francisco Chronicle*, January 2, 2008, A1, 14.

11. Brian Handwerk, "Wind Turbines Give Bats the 'Bends,' Study Finds," *National Georgraphic News*, August 25, 2008. Available at http://news.national geographic.com/news/pf/61204214.html.

12. "Bat Fatalities at Wind Turbines: Investigating the Causes and Consequences," *Fort Collins Science Center USGS*. Available at http://www.fort.usgs.gov/BatsWindmills/.

13. See note 9 above.

14. Ladislaus Rybach, "Geothermal Energy: Sustainability and the Environment," *Geothermics* 32 (2003): 467. Available at http://www.sciencedirect.com/science?

15. John W. Lund, Derek H. Freeston, Tonya L. Boyd, "Direct Application of Geothermal Energy: 2005 Worldwide Review," *Geothermics* 34 (2005); 723. Available at http://www.sciencedirect.com/science?. Also

see Burkhard Sanner, Constantine Karytsas, Dimitrios Mendrinos, Ladislaus Rybach, "Current Status of Ground Source Heat Pumps and Underground Thermal Energy Storage in Europe," *Geothermics* 32 (2003): 579–88. Available at http://www.sciencedirect.com/science?.

16. Lund, Freeston, Boyd, "Direct Application of Geothermal Energy," 692.

17. Arne Kildegaard and Josephine Myers-Kuykindall, "Community vs. Corporate Wind: Does It Matter Who Develops the Wind in Big Stone County, MN?" Research prepared in fulfillment of IREE grant no. SGP4C2004, Department of Economics, University of Minnesota Morris, Morris, MN 56267. Revised September 2006, pp. 1, 3. A link for this research is available at http://www.windustry.com/communitywind.

18. Farmers' Legal Action Group (FLAG), "Reaching Community Wind's Potential," March, 2007, 5. A link for this article is available at http://www.windustry.com/communitywind.

19. Ibid.

20. Ibid., 1, 2.

21. Kildegaard and Myers-Kuykindall, "Community vs. Corporate Wind," 8. This discussion referred to research prepared for the Energy Trusts of Oregon cited in M. Bolinger, R. Wiser, T. Wind, D. Juhl, and R. Grace, "A Comparative Analysis of Community Wind Power Development Options in Oregon," Portland, Ore., 2004.

INDEX OF NAMES AND SUBJECTS